Bizarre Fantasy Football XI's

DAVID KOHN

David Martin Kohn was born, the middle of three brothers, in Middlesbrough in the early 1960s. Short-sighted, skinny and excessively cowardly, David was often excused from games as an infant. He used the time well, developing one of the world's finest mental libraries of useless trivia. This strange child did not dream of becoming a racing driver, he dreamed of becoming President of the Association of Football Statisticians.

In his teens, David developed his skills further, branching out into more esoteric fields of trivia – cricketers' initials, ground attendance records and car number-plate designations among others. During this time he did not have a girlfriend.

Aged 21, he finally talked to a woman and romance blossomed when he realised she knew more about football than he did. She is now a man. Eventually he found a job and he has, after many years of effort, successfully managed his way to the middle. His career peaked at the age of 25, when he was mistaken for someone else and promoted. He has since been shunted sideways more times than Steve Coppell.

He is now happily married with three kids, each of whom is named after a favourite Boro player. Alan (Foggon) and Spike (Armstrong) are happy enough, but Juninho takes a fearful ribbing at school, especially as she's a girl.

Now reduced by age to armchair spectating, David's specialist subject is 'Where to find what on the Ceefax sports pages'. He handles his remote control like a teenager handles a Playstation Console.

His only remaining ambition – for Middlesbrough FC to bring back both manager Jack Charlton and the classic 1973/74 strip with the 'lucky' white band across the chest. Oh, and to score the winning goal in a Cup Final … aw, come on, Roger Osborne did.

Bizarre Fantasy Football XI's

BY DAVID KOHN

DEDICATIONS

To Dawn for understanding my insanity and not encouraging me to change

To Samuel, Anna and Jacob – hopefully you'll grow up to be immature enough to enjoy this

To John Hickton – never given the international recognition you deserved

ACKNOWLEDGEMENTS

Special thanks to Tim Vigon

Thanks to all at Generation, especially Paul Sudbury, Phil McNeill,
Eve Cossins, Mark Crossland, Joseph Crowe and Clare Warde

To Graham Edmonds because you asked for a credit

To Dave Crowe for encouraging me to do it

And to every bloke in every pub I've ever had a conversation with

Design by Generation Studio

Published by David Crowe and Mark Peacock

All photographs courtesy of Allsport
apart from Empics (78, 84), Mirror Syndication
International (56, 57) and Popperfoto (18, 19)

First published in Great Britain in 1999 by
Generation Publications Limited
11-12 Tottenham Mews
London W1P 9PJ

generationgroup@btconnect.com

CIP data for this title is available from the British Library

ISBN 1 90300918 9

Reprographics by Media Print (UK) Ltd

Printed and bound in Spain by Boookprint, S.L., Barcelona

Welcome to the BIZARRE

Foreword

BY RON ATKINSON

If the concept of 22 grown men getting paid several million quid to chase around a field after a leather ball isn't bizarre enough for you, this book serves to remind football fans everywhere that when it comes to bizarre, the wonderful world of football has it all – nutters, hard men, boozers, fat lads, baldies, mavericks and the just plain useless… And I should know because I reckon I've worked with at least half the guys mentioned in this book at some time or other.

Chuck in bad hair, bad attitude, bad decisions, bad buys, bad boys and you end up with some pretty wild team combinations that prove football's crazy, definitely, but boring, never.

What's more, if I told someone outside of football some of the stories and anecdotes printed here I doubt anyone would believe

'When it comes to bizarre, football has it all. I should know – I've worked with half the guys in this book'

me – at least I can now point at the printed page and say "I told you so."

I wouldn't be drawn by the author into giving my recommendations for any of the fantasy teams listed here, even though I've never been known for being shy when it comes to opinions on players. I may have hung up the sheepskin now, but you never know when or where that next tempting job offer might come from…

So, enjoy this playful romp through popular football culture and remember that despite its intentions and pretensions, there's always a laugh or two to be had when, as it so often does, the Premiership season becomes the pantomime season. (Yes, I've played the genie a few times.)

As they say, it's a funny old game…

Ron Atkinson

They seek Big Ron...

Sheffield Wednesday

just about everywhere

Aston Villa

MAVERICK XI

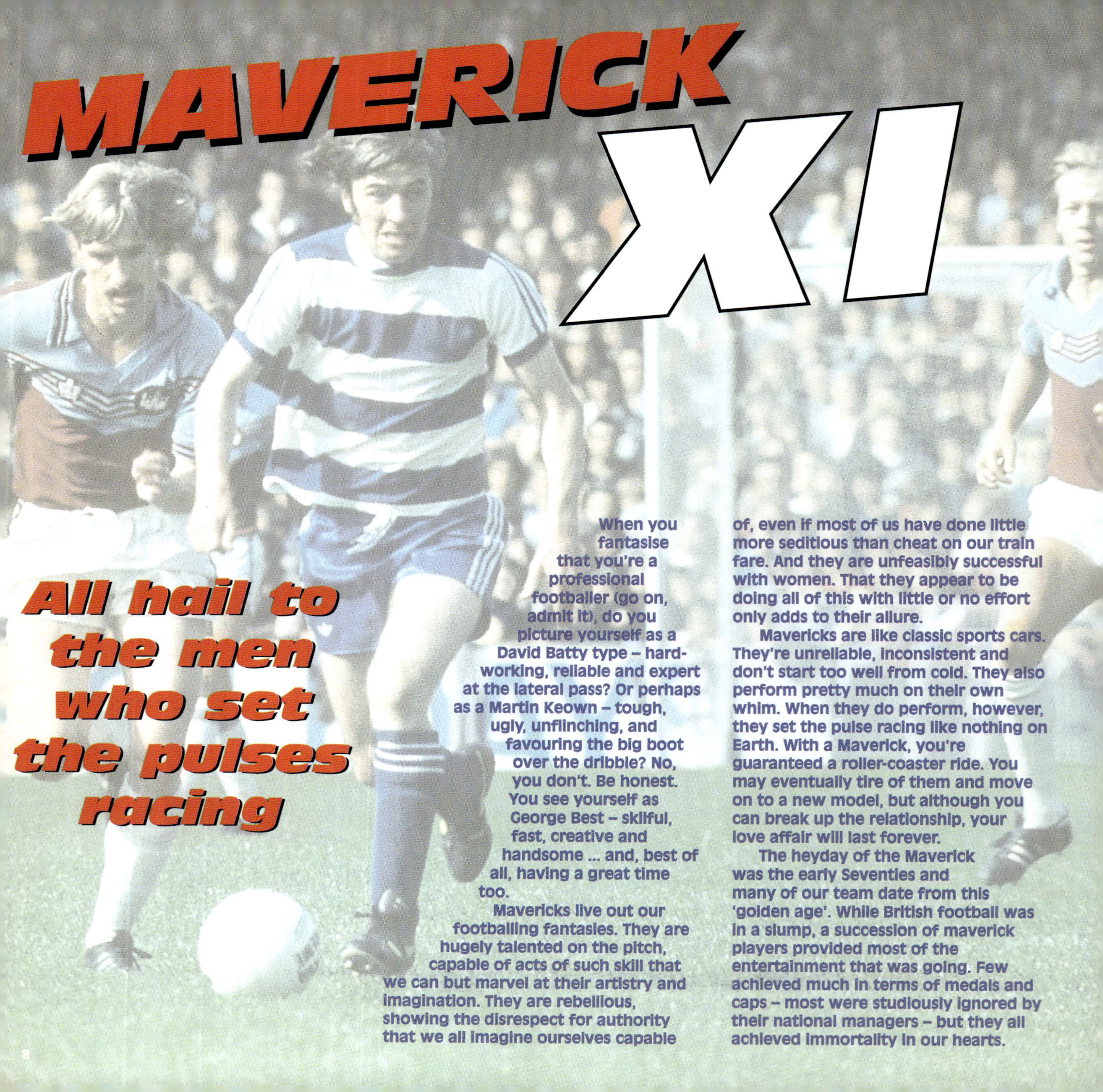

All hail to the men who set the pulses racing

When you fantasise that you're a professional footballer (go on, admit it), do you picture yourself as a David Batty type – hard-working, reliable and expert at the lateral pass? Or perhaps as a Martin Keown – tough, ugly, unflinching, and favouring the big boot over the dribble? No, you don't. Be honest. You see yourself as George Best – skilful, fast, creative and handsome ... and, best of all, having a great time too.

Mavericks live out our footballing fantasies. They are hugely talented on the pitch, capable of acts of such skill that we can but marvel at their artistry and imagination. They are rebellious, showing the disrespect for authority that we all imagine ourselves capable of, even if most of us have done little more seditious than cheat on our train fare. And they are unfeasibly successful with women. That they appear to be doing all of this with little or no effort only adds to their allure.

Mavericks are like classic sports cars. They're unreliable, inconsistent and don't start too well from cold. They also perform pretty much on their own whim. When they do perform, however, they set the pulse racing like nothing on Earth. With a Maverick, you're guaranteed a roller-coaster ride. You may eventually tire of them and move on to a new model, but although you can break up the relationship, your love affair will last forever.

The heyday of the Maverick was the early Seventies and many of our team date from this 'golden age'. While British football was in a slump, a succession of maverick players provided most of the entertainment that was going. Few achieved much in terms of medals and caps – most were studiously ignored by their national managers – but they all achieved immortality in our hearts.

Maverick XI

Roberto Carlos could crack a Brazil nut between those thighs

BRUCE GROBBELAAR

Bruce Grobbelaar, with his Village People moustache, Zimbabwean army background and extrovert goalkeeping, has always stood out from the pack. Prone to mistakes Grobbelaar was nevertheless a highly effective keeper who got his hands on more silverware than most top cat-burglers. Bob Paisley, no less, rated him the best in Britain.
Best moment: Going all wobbly-kneed to put off the Roma penalty-takers in the 1984 European Cup Final.
Best gag: Arsenal fans waving tenners at him after the match-rigging allegations and singing "Brucie, Brucie, give us a goal."
Clubs: Vancouver, Crewe, Liverpool, Stoke, S'thampton, Plymouth, Oldham, Bury, Lincoln.
Record: League games 539; Goals 1; Zimbabwe caps 20.

STAN BOWLES (opposite)

Stan Bowles epitomises the Seventies maverick. Drink, drugs, women, an excessive amount of gambling ... oh, and a little football as well. Bowles was thought by many contemporaries to have been the best of them all – fantastic control, great dribbling skills, plenty of goals. Compared to most mavericks, he was also an unselfish team player. He and Gerry Francis drove QPR to untold heights in the 1970s.

But Bowles was also the ultimate bloke, getting into all manner of scrapes. Gambling was his main weakness and he would often be seen during a game sidling up to the terraces to get the result of the 3:30 or 4:10. Rumour has it Stan would sometimes get himself stretchered off so he could run down to the bookies and catch the last race.

Stan, in common with other mavericks, played few (only five) times for his country. After his third game, in which he felt he was unjustly substituted, he walked out of the England squad. It was clear that Stan had bigger priorities. A few hours after walking out on England he was spotted at the White City dog track. It was really no contest.
Best moment: The winning goal against Leeds, in the final game of the 1975/6 season to put QPR (for nine heady days) on top.
Teams: Man City, Bury (loan), Crewe, Carlisle, QPR, Forest, Orient, Brentford.
Record: League appearances 506; goals 127; England caps 5; goals 1.

ROBERTO CARLOS

Roberto Carlos has unusually large and muscular thighs that he apparently dotes on. The thighs not only look great (to Roberto) but also enable outrageous free kicks like his amazing banana goal against France in 1997. As a full-back he has won more plaudits for his attacking play than his defending and this marks him out as a modern-day maverick. He just can't resist getting forward.
Best moment: That free kick. It set off towards the corner flag, ran almost parallel to the goal-line before swerving left and into the goal.

JIMMY JOHNSTONE

Like many Scottish players of his generation, 'Jinky' Jimmy Johnstone liked a drink or seven when the opportunity presented itself. After one infamous session, Johnstone found himself alone on a boat heading out to sea without any oars – literally up shit creek without a paddle. The drunken attempts of his team-mates to rescue him came to naught and he was eventually rescued by two local boatmen who responded to a police SOS.

Best moment: Against Leeds United in the European Cup Semi-Final 1967. "What he did to Terry Cooper should be prohibited by Act of Parliament." – Jim Baxter

DUNCAN McKENZIE

Duncan McKenzie was famed in the early Seventies for two things: first, his smoking habit – he puffed his way through 40 a day – and second, his mastery of the rare art of Mini-jumping – he could allegedly achieve this in one leap.

McKenzie became Leeds United's most expensive player in 1974 when he was signed by Brian Clough – itself an achievement, as Clough stayed at Leeds a mere 44 days – but he never really settled after leaving his first club, Nottingham Forest. Despite much popular acclaim (and occasional frustration) the mercurial Mr McKenzie was never selected to play for his country, thus becoming one of the best players never to play for England.

Teams: Nottingham Forest, Mansfield (loan), Leeds, Anderlecht, Everton, Chelsea, Blackburn Rovers.

Record: League appearances 330; goals 112.

JIM BAXTER

Baxter established himself as a legend at Rangers, winning the double in 1963 then the treble in 1964 before moving south to Sunderland in 1965. A constant thorn in England's side, his record against the Auld Enemy was played five, won four, including two famous wins at Wembley. Still, he was as famous for his brushes with authority and for his excesses – booze and birds – as he was for his football.

Best moment: Tormenting the English at Wembley in 1963 to lead Scotland to a famous 2-1 win

Quote: "Scandal came easy to him, it was simply a way of life" – Stuart Cosgrove, Hampden Babylon

Teams: Raith Rovers, Rangers, Sunderland, Forest, Rangers.

Record: Scotland caps 34; goals 3.

CHARLIE GEORGE

Charlie George was the classic Norf London, North Bank boy made good. Growing up within spitting distance of Highbury, and coming through the youth scheme, Charlie became the terrace hero at Arsenal. At a time when Arsenal (astonishingly) were considered really quite dull, Charlie was a cavalier who always looked to do the unpredictable. He never really fulfilled the promise of his youth, but will be forever remembered for the best FA Cup Final goal celebration of all time and, quite possibly, the worst haircut.

Finest moment: 1971 FA Cup Final and that celebration

Teams: Arsenal, Derby, Southampton, Forest, Bulova (HK), Bournemouth, Derby

Record: League appearances 298; goals 78; England caps 1.

Charlie George: No friend of the barber

Training? I'm a footballer, not a bloody sea lion!

Paul McGrath: A legend in his own lifetime, especially at lunchtimes, after work, and no doubt at late lock-ins

PAUL McGRATH

Paul McGrath is a modern-day hero. On the pitch the centre-back has defied two famously dodgy knees and a seemingly total aversion to training to play with distinction for Man U, Villa and the Republic of Ireland – becoming the Republic's most capped player. His reading of the game bears comparison with that of the great Bobby Moore. Off the pitch, his drinking is legendary, with sprees featuring Messrs Robson, Whiteside and McGrath entering footballing myth. A great example to us all.

Finest moment: Going AWOL before a World Cup qualifying tie with Albania.

Teams: Man U, Villa, Derby, Sheffield United.

Record: League appearances 452; goals 21; Eire caps 83; goals 8.

FRANK WORTHINGTON

Worthington was a great under-achiever. In a career spanning 22 years, he won only two Second Division championships and eight caps. He did, however, entertain fans at 11 clubs – and women in most of the towns of England. With his sideburns, cowboy outfits and love of Elvis, he never took himself seriously and was much loved by many fans.

Clubs: Huddersfield, Leicester, Bolton, Birmingham, Leeds, Southampton, Brighton, Tranmere, Preston, Stockport.

Record: League games 757; Goals 234; England caps 8; Goals 2.

RODNEY MARSH

Pele said Rodney Marsh was "English, but he plays like a Brazilian". Marsh entertained crowds regally in the late Sixties/early Seventies. His 'don't give a fuck' attitude made him vastly popular with fans, but he was not universally admired by fellow players and managers. As Frank McLintock said: "The trouble with Marshy was he'd rather put the ball through someone's legs than score a goal."

Finest moment: Hat-trick for QPR vs Birmingham in 1970.

Teams: Fulham, QPR, Man City, Tampa Bay Rowdies, Fulham.

Record: League appearances 408; goals 169; England caps 9; goals 1.

PETER OSGOOD

Osgood was the glamour player for the glamour side of English football in the early Seventies, Chelsea. Though they didn't win much – FA Cup in 1970 and Cup Winners' Cup in '71 – they were many people's second-favourite side in this period and were certainly the celebrities' choice. Osgood stood out not only for having three O's in his name but also for his supreme confidence, showmanship and scoring ability – on and off the pitch.

Peter's Colgate ad audition

Finest moment: Diving header to equalise vs Leeds in 1970 FA Cup Final replay.

Teams: Chelsea, Southampton, Norwich (loan), Philadelphia, Chelsea.

Record: League games 418; goals 133; England caps 4.

Left: The Cruyff turn.
Right: The Cruyff dummy...

JOHANN CRUYFF

Cruyff led Ajax to three European Cups, made Holland the best team in the world and, best of all, invented the Cruyff turn, imitated but never mastered by footballers the world over. He was an intelligent and complex character who was often at war with his coaches and directors. He was always convinced he was right – and usually was!

Clubs: Ajax, Barcelona, LA Aztecs, Washington Diplomats, Levante, Ajax, Feyenoord. **Main honours:** European Cup 1971, 1972, 1973; European Footballer of the Year 1971, 1973, 1974

'I always had a reputation for going missing. Miss England, Miss United Kingdom, Miss World...'
– George Best

STAR PLAYER PROFILE

GEORGE BEST

Born: May 22, 1946, Belfast
Teams: Man Utd, Stockport (loan), LA Aztecs, Fulham, Golden Bay, Bournemouth
Record: League games 411; goals 37; Northern Ireland caps 37; goals 9

George Best: Always keen to score

1961 Joins Manchester United as an amateur, aged 15.
1963 Signs as pro on 17th birthday; makes debut in September in a 1-0 home win vs West Brom.
1964 Makes debut for Northern Ireland in 3-2 win vs Wales.
1965 Wins first league championship.
1966 Scores two great goals in what was possibly the best game of his career, the 5-1 away win against Benfica in the European Cup quarter-final.
1967 Wins second league championship.
1968 Scores twice in United's historic 4-1 victory vs Benfica in the European Cup Final; voted domestic Footballer of the Year and European Footballer of the Year.
1970 Suspended for four weeks for kicking ball out of referee Jack Taylor's hands. Best returns for fifth-round FA Cup tie against aspirant giant-killers Northampton, and scores six in an 8-2 win. Drops back with 15 minutes remaining so as not to totally humiliate the opposition.
1972 The day before his 26th birthday, George announces his retirement. This will not be his last...
1974 After a succession of retirements and comebacks, makes his last appearance for United in a New Year's Day 3-0 defeat to QPR. Best, by this stage, is well down the slippery slope, drinking and gambling to excess.
1975 Plays three games for Stockport in the Fourth Division – attendances rocket.
1976 Signs for Fulham from LA Aztecs – scores within 71 seconds of debut; within a month becomes one of the first players to receive a red card.
1978 Last of 37 appearances for Northern Ireland; becomes irregular, itinerant footballer.
1981 Checks into alcohol clinic for first time ... it will not be his last.
1984 Spends Christmas at Her Majesty's pleasure following drunk driving episode.
1990 Writes his autobiography – ***The Good, The Bad and The Bubbly.*** Makes legendary appearance on ***Wogan*** while blind drunk.
1999 Still (somehow) alive – and still a legend.

WORD UP

'Kevin Keegan isn't fit to lace my boots.'
– George Best
'Keegan isn't fit to lace Best's drinks.'
– John Roberts

Chopper Harris always took a memento of every tackle

Who ATE ALL THE PIES XI

Razor Ruddock: Football hard man and fat bastard. (Uh-oh, looks like he heard that...)

Throughout the years, members of the British footballing public have kept a Desperate Dan-sized place in their affections for the more rotund members of the playing profession. Rather than deride these poor examples of athleticism as the lazy sluggards that proper criticism demands, fans have tended to take these players to their hearts.

There are doubtless good psychological reasons for this. Perhaps watching players with excess body fat makes us feel that little bit less inadequate when we view our own flabby physique in the mirror. Maybe seeing fat people perform at the highest sporting level gives us the hope that we too could do it. Possibly it is the classic British identification with the loser.

But the explanation may be more socio-logical. In Britain, the amateur ethos retains a strong hold. Our abiding national character-istic is that we love to think we can win without really trying. Take training, for example. Until recently, the classic British training session consisted of five laps round the pitch, a few shuttle runs and a session of pot shots at the YTS trainee in goal. This was then topped up by three hours' snooker, a visit to Ladbroke's to put thirty sovs on the 3:40 at Newbury, and a trip to the museum to see the latest exhibition of Egyptian antiquities (alright, that last one was made up). It was hardly surprising we lost to continental sides ... the buggers trained twice a day and didn't even drink beer!

Or take tactics. For several years the Director of National Coaching in England was a gentleman by the name of Charles Hughes. Hughes was passionate in his advocacy of 'direct football' or the 'long ball game'. To have used more sophisticated tactics would have smacked of thinking about it, and we didn't want to appear to the rest of the world to be taking the game seriously.

Yes, in Britain we've clung resolutely to the belief that we could win, it's just that we don't really take it that seriously. The fat footballer is one of the best manifestations of this and as such is placed on a pedestal (obviously a sturdy one). We love these players, because they reinforce our misplaced confidence that if only we bother to try as hard as the others we'd be world-beaters.

Subs bench
Bobby Murdoch
Jamie Pollock

Mick Quinn: Caution wide load

NEIL RUDDOCK

A terrace hero wherever he has played, Neil 'Razor' Ruddock is aggressive, strong and gutsy. Well, he certainly showed a lot of gut in his last few appearances for Liverpool. A self-proclaimed hard man / nutter, Ruddock was brought to Liverpool by Graeme Souness to add some weight to the team – and he certainly did that. He looks the sort who is likely to balloon when he gives up the game, so it seems inevitable that the Razor will be blunted.
Vital statistics: Height 6'2"; weight 12st 12 lb (unchanged since 1993 … ahem)

LARRY LLOYD

Laurence (whisper it softly) Valentine Lloyd won only four caps for England but was a commanding defender who enjoyed success with Liverpool and Nottingham Forest. Always on the large side as a player, it is as a publican that he has really excelled in the lard stakes. As Brian Clough notes in his autobiography: "After years in the pub trade he is now almost as big as the bloody Castle. Whenever I see him I worry that he's about to burst." Rare praise from the maestro.
Vital statistics: Height 6'2"; weight hmmm…

JAMIE POLLOCK (Sub)

It's hard to believe now, but Jamie Pollock was once considered to have a big future ahead of him. Now he's got a big behind behind him. As captain of England U-19s, he was touted as the next Bryan Robson. He proved to have more in common with Bryan the snail from the Magic Roundabout. Pollock certainly carries extra weight and his lack of pace is such that he was once unable to get out the way of a car … that was being push-started.
Vital statistics: Height 5'11"; weight 14st.

JOHN ROBERTSON

When Brian Clough arrived at Nottingham Forest in 1975, John Robertson was on the transfer list. As Clough describes it, it wasn't difficult to see why. He was "a habitual smoker, possibly ten pounds overweight, indisputably the slowest player in the Football League … he was fat, often unshaven, dressed like a tramp, and smoked one fag after another".

Robertson, however, had talent in abundance and in Clough he found a manager to help him realise that talent. He was a key player in the Championship-winning side of 1977/78, crossed the killer ball for Trevor Francis to win the European Cup in 1979 and scored the winner himself against Hamburg in 1980. All on top of 28 caps for Scotland.

Not bad for someone described by Clough (again) as "a slob, an absolute slob".
Vital statistics: Height 5'8"; weight 10st 9 lb (oh really?)

Who Ate All The Pies XI

Julian mistakenly thought a goatee would make him look slim

JULIAN DICKS

An uncannily similar profile to Ruddock – loved by the fans for his old-fashioned commitment and hard tackling – he has made Upton Park his own despite being a Bristolian by birth and upbringing.

His rotund period coincided with a brief, unhappy stay at Liverpool – where (like Ruddock) he was brought in by Souness. Was it homesickness for the Hammers that led to excessive comfort eating by the amusingly named Dicks? Poor lamb.

Vital statistics: Height 5'10"; weight 13 st.

FRANCIS LEE

Once upon a time Manchester City had a good football team – a very good team in fact. They won the League in 1968, the FA Cup in 1969, and the Cup Winners' and League Cups in 1970.

Their attack was led by a short, barrel-chested, highly combative centre-forward who scored at the rate of a goal every other game – Frannie Lee. Lee's magic touch deserted him as chairman of the club, but as a player he remains a hero to the City faithful.

Vital statistics: Height 5'7"; weight 12 st 2 lb.

MICK QUINN

Standing only 5'9", not blessed with natural pace and carrying a top-class beer gut, Mickey Quinn should never have made it as a top-class footballer. But make it he did, with over 200 League goals testament to his innate ability to sniff out a chance and convert it into a goal.

In common with Greaves and Muller, Quinn was not the most natural of athletes but was certainly one of the most natural of finishers.

Vital statistics: Height 5'9"; weight 13 st.

SAMMY LEE

"He's fat, he's round, he's worth a million pound, Sammy Lee, Sammy Lee" was a chant that resounded around Anfield from 1977 to '85. It was technically correct on two counts. Lee was never particularly popular outside Merseyside – he was like an early version of David Batty but without the creativity – but he managed to win more medals than a Chelsea pensioner and to gain 13 caps for England, even scoring twice. He was also the last man called Sammy to play for England.

Vital statistics: Height 5'6"; weight too much.

ARCHIE GEMMILL

Archibald Gemmill is the unlikely scorer of two of the greatest goals of all time. Nottingham Forest v Arsenal 1977/8 – a flowing, length-of-the-pitch movement climaxing in Gemmill's sliding tap-in – and, of course, Scotland vs Holland in the 1978 World Cup. Gemmill's jinking run and deadly near-post finish are famous the world over, more so after the goal was used to comic effect in the film ***Trainspotting***. Yes, short, fat, balding men can become film stars, too.

Vital statistics: Height 5'5"; weight 11 st 2 lb.

PAUL GASCOIGNE

Middlesbrough fans have had a hard time of things lately. Three losing Cup Finals in two years, relegation from the Premiership and a string of dodgy foreign signings. The icing on the cake came in March 1998 with the signing of Paul 'Mars Bar Kid' Gascoigne. A fee of £3.45 million and salary of £1.5 million a year can only have been based on a £ per kilo measurement. For all the weighty words about Gazza getting back in the England XI, he didn't even make the Boro top XI for the 1998/99 season.

Vital statistics: Height 5'10"; weight 11 st 10 lb (in his dreams).

BOBBY MURDOCH (Sub)

England probably didn't see the best of Bobby Murdoch when he left his beloved Celtic to play for Jack Charlton's Middlesbrough in 1973. The European Cup winner of 1967 was still an intelligent player, but he needed all of this intelligence given his profound lack of pace. He occupied space (a lot of it) in midfield and managed to look like a dad out for a Sunday afternoon. It was no shock when he ended up running a pub.

Vital statistics: Height 5'10"; weight 12 st 8 lb.

JAN MOLBY

Jan the Man is, alongside Peter Schmeichel and bacon, one of Denmark's three most valued exports to the UK. An assimilated Brit now, he has a flawless scouse accent (apparently used by Harry Enfield as the model for his Scousers sketch), a criminal record and a whole load of gambling debts and financial troubles. All we'd expect from a British pro and more.

Jan always appeared to be an unusual shape for a footballer – his torso sticks out like the prow of a tall ship – and he was noted neither for his pace nor his workrate. His skill and vision, however, were of true class, so we excused him this and his off-the-field indiscretions, too. Jan has been through a lot – certainly a lot of food – but he is a one-off and we should treasure him.

Vital statistics: Height 6'2"; weight 15 st 10 lb (now we're talking).

'Here lads, don't try and grab my sausage at half-time'

Sammy Lee: Mmmmmm, sexy shorts

FATTY FOULKE WIDE BO

The England star who made Gazza look anorexic

Watch footage of football from the early part of the century and several things stand out:

- The slow pace of the game (or is it that film was slower then?)
- The unimpeded dribbling, as though tackling of skilful players was banned
- The uniformity of the crowd's dress – would sir like a flat cap and rattle?
- And, most pertinently, the laughably poor standard of goalkeeping.

William 'Fatty' Foulke was the standard-bearer for keepers in this era. A man who at his peak topped the scales at 22 stone, he was nevertheless deemed good enough to gain a cap for England and, for the record, to keep a clean sheet.

His strengths were that forwards found it excessively time-consuming getting round him in a one-on-one situation, and that he occupied about half of the goal's surface area. He seemed to understand this, and had a sense of humour, apparently being quoted as saying: "I don't mind what you call me as long as you don't call me late for dinner."

DY!

***William 'Fatty' Foulke:** Also known as 'Little Willie', Foulke was captain of Chelsea – though perhaps not the most popular person to fill that role as he once ate all 11 players' breakfasts. After 347 League appearances, he became a beach entertainer in Blackpool, where he challenged trippers to score penalties against him. He died from pneumonia aged 41*

PLEASE TELL ME I DIDN'T JUST DO THAT XI

Gazza showing his typical diplomacy

Footballers today are continuously under the spotlight. On the pitch, all matches in the Premiership and Nationwide Leagues are now filmed, and sometimes, expensively in John Hartson's case, training ground incidents too. Things that players have got away with for years are now seized upon, highlighted and replayed in gruesome detail. Take the Fowler-Le Saux incident. Not only can you see what happened from three angles, but you also have the benefit of Andy Gray's magic pen identifying the exact trajectory of Le Saux's elbow and pinpointing the precise point of impact on Fowler's extensive conk.

Off the pitch, players can't rest either. Immediately after a game they might be asked how they feel about the result. They can't say what we would – "I'm f***ing pissed off!" or "That cheating ref bastard" – instead they have to be diplomatic and congratulate the opposition – probably the last thing they want to do at that point in time.

Then later on they might go out to relax. Not a chance. Step out of line and someone is bound to catch up with you. One night Gazza's having an innocent pint and a kebab at 3:00 in the morning, the next day the press are all over him as though he's not taking his training seriously.

It's no wonder that so few footballers put their heads above the parapet to say or do anything interesting any more. Thankfully, though, not all of them have been trained in the rules of PR, or if they have, they have quickly forgotten them. These unfortunates are the subject of this team, the players who have wittingly or unwittingly caused upset to the great British football public. If you're easily offended, look away now...

Insults XI

'And now for my Basil Fawlty impression...' (Oh really, Mark?)

MARK BOSNICH

In January 1995 Mark Bosnich made an attempt (or so it seemed) on the life of Tottenham striker Jurgen Klinsmann. In an aerial challenge reminiscent of Schumacher on Battiston in 1982, Bosnich hurled himself at Klinsmann rendering the German unconscious and unable to play on.

Spurs fans were none too happy and took it out on Bosnich on his next couple of visits to White Hart Lane. On the second of these, in October 1996, Bosnich responded to the crowd's relentless booing with a Nazi salute and goose step. Given that many Spurs fans are Jewish, this was considered somewhat insensitive. Bosnich's subsequent apologies – live from the team bus on Radio 5's *606 Show* – were embarrassing for their sincerity.

He claimed he was only doing a Basil Fawlty impersonation. If only it had been Sybil, he would have been OK.

NIGEL WINTERBURN

'Giving the finger' to opposition fans is a gesture that could be seen by some to be offensive. In a London derby away from home it might be seen as inflammatory. When the fans concerned are disabled, it takes on a whole new meaning.

Arsenal's left-back reputedly celebrated his last-minute winner against Chelsea by gesturing in such a manner to the front-row wheelchair fraternity. Nothing was proven, but rumour has it that several wheelchairs in the King's Road are now kitted out with red-and-white-seeking missile launchers.

Right: Nigel 'Nutty Boy' Winterburn

FRANK RIJKAARD
(above with Rudi Voller)

Holland vs Germany is always a combustible affair. The Dutch still remember the War and their occupation by the Germans. The Germans ... well, who cares what they think?

In 1990 the two countries met in Milan in the second round of the World Cup. In the second half Rijkaard fouled Rudi Voller, who dived; the ref showed Rijkaard the yellow card, which meant he would be suspended for the next match; Rijkaard then went after Voller, producing two of the largest volleys of spit ever seen on a football field and landing them both in Voller's hair. Both players were sent off, Voller for no apparent reason – although the ref later revealed it was for possessing an offensive hairstyle.

The mild-mannered Rijkaard had no real explanation for his behaviour. Perhaps, though, he was venting the frustration that all of us feel when Germany manage to luck their way through to another bloody title.

LEE CLARK

A lifelong Newcastle fan, Lee Clark was accepted by the Sunderland fans as long as he did the business on the park, which he managed consistently last season. He rather blotted his copybook, however, when photographed before this year's FA Cup final sporting a T-shirt carrying the slogan 'Sad Mackem Bastards'. As he plays for the said 'Sad Mackem Bastards', this could be considered something of an error of judgement. Result – Clark now on the transfer list; family now in hiding.

STEFAN EFFENBERG (below)

Effenberg has always been his own man, continually falling out with management and moving clubs when the mood suits. Effenberg was substituted during Germany's poor performance against South Korea in WC 1994 and booed by his own fans as he came off the pitch. His middle-finger gesture saw him sent home in disgrace and he has not played for his country since.

SAVO MILOSEVIC

Despite his wonder goal in the '96 Coca-Cola Cup Final, Savo Milosevic was never truly accepted by the Villa fans. Perhaps it had something to do with sharing a name with one of Europe's most hated men. Or perhaps it was just his innate ineptitude.

Whatever it was, he well and truly burned his bridges when, in an away game at Blackburn (eventually lost 0-5), he went over to the Villa fans and visibly spat at them. Surprisingly, he didn't win the Supporters' Player of the Season award that year and he was soon on his way not only out of Villa but also out of the country.

BILLY BREMNER & KEVIN KEEGAN

The Charity Shield of 1974 brought together the two best sides in England, Liverpool and Leeds, for a supposed friendly. The match got off to a bad start when, in the opening minute, Alan Clarke put his foot into a tackle with Phil Thompson, thus prompting a series of niggling fouls from both sides.

Johnny Giles – a notorious niggler – put in a couple of fouls on Keegan, then topped them with a career-threatener. As the ref was sorting it out, Bremner came over to suggest that Keegan had dived.

Result – fisticuffs and two of Britain's best players sent off at Wembley. Both then staged a silent protest by removing their shirts. Result – 11-match bans for both and proof that Bremner was a natural 'ginga'.

IAN CROOK

Alright, so it's not Rangers-Celtic or Barcelona-Real Madrid, but when Ipswich play Norwich the East Anglian locals can get excited enough to stop looking admiringly at their pigs for 90 minutes. When Norwich gave playmaker Ian Crook a free transfer in 1996 he was delighted when Ipswich offered him a contract. Before he joined the enemy, however, Mike Walker returned to Carrow Road and offered Crook a coaching job.

Crook swiftly did an about-turn and returned to Norwich without actually ever leaving. His popularity was damaged, however – In Ipswich they hated him for spurning them; in Norwich they hated him for thinking of going to Ipswich in the first place. Best find somewhere out west, Ian.

SAMMY NELSON

'Mooning' has always held a strange fascination for men, and most of us have at some stage performed the act – normally when seated at the rear of a coach – in front of unwitting and unwilling spectators. It shouldn't be funny, but it is.

The classic football 'moon' was by Sammy Nelson of Arsenal in a home match against Coventry in April 1979. Nelson had scored an own goal in the first half and the home crowd were giving him stick. Ever keen to entertain the locals, the full-back dropped his kaks and showed them the big brown eye. The match finished 1-1. Typical Arse-nal.

CANTONA, KUNG FU KING

January 25, 1995. Manchester United travel to Selhurst Park to take on lowly Crystal Palace. United have three days earlier recorded a critical win against leaders Blackburn Rovers, courtesy of a goal from a certain Monsieur Eric Cantona, and need only to win to go top of the table. The rest is history.

Cantona is sent off for a rash challenge on Richard Shaw. He angrily leaves the pitch with the great peacemaker Paul Ince in close attendance. Some of the crowd abuse is a trifle over the top. Before we know it, Cantona has launched himself into the crowd with an authentic two-footed kung fu kick and fists are flying. Police move in and the whole incident is over without anyone really noticing. (OK, so that last bit is not strictly true.)

Cantona was banned for eight months and sentenced to 120 hours' community service; Matthew Simmons, a rather unpleasant thug from South London, had his 15 minutes of fame but was banned by Palace for life; Man U failed to win the Premiership; and Eric gave the world his thoughts about seagulls and trawlers.

'I would have cut off his testicles.'
– Steady on, Mr Clough

'I don't think anyone in the history of football will get the sentence Eric's got unless they'd killed Bert Millichip's dog.'
– A typically contrite Alex Ferguson

STAR PLAYER PROFILE

Teams: Auxerre, Marseille, Bordeaux, Montpellier, Nîmes, Leeds, Manchester United.
League appearances 171; Goals 73.
Honours: League title (Leeds 1992), 4 Premiership titles (Man Utd 1993, 1994, 1996, 1997); FA Cup 1994, 1996.

AAH Cantona!

*'THE SH*T HITS THE FAN'*
– Daily Star headline

'OOH, AAH, PRISONAA!'
– Sun headline after court case

*'Ooh, aah, French w**ka!'*
– West Ham fans' chant

Please Tell Me I Didn't Just Do That!

Gaz

Paul Gascoigne is not considered to be a very bright bloke. Nor a very mature one. His capacity to inflict damage on himself through insensitivity and PR blunders is matched only by Prince Philip. The evidence ...

1990 – Having won the hearts of the nation with his talent and tears in Italia '90, he appeared on the airplane steps wearing what can only be described as a pair of comedy plastic breasts. Class.

1992 – Playing for Lazio in Rome, Gazza is asked a question about the match by one of the country's most respected journalists. His answer: to burp into the microphone on national TV. Just plain genius.

1993 – In Norway for a vital WC qualifying match he was asked if he had a message for the people of Norway. His reply was succinct: 'Yes I do – F**k off Norway.' Quality.

1995 – Gascoigne marks his first Rangers-Celtic derby by miming the flute-playing of the Protestant Orangemen. Exclaiming 'The Pope is a c**t' would have been less inflammatory. Just plain stupid.

1998 – On the eve of the World Cup, with Glenn Hoddle about to name his final squad, Gazza is desperate to prove his fitness. He does so by going out on the beer with Danny Baker and Chris Evans and finishing off the evening with a doner kebab. Gazza – you're a twat!

zza

'The doctor at Lazio told me I should try drinking wine, because it would be good for me. When I did, he took one look at me and said: "You'd better go back on the beer".'

ROBBIE 'THE LAD' FOWLER

Robbie Fowler has never come across as one of football's Masterminds. He looks like the sort of kid who, if he weren't playing footie, would spend most of his time playing pool, driving round in a beat-up Ford Escort and shoplifting from Woolworths. In short, he is a lad.

Nineteen ninety-nine showed Robbie in his true colours. On February 27 he very publicly showed us what he thought of Graeme Le Saux's sexuality. His schoolboy mime certainly riled Graeme, whose elbow connected very nicely with Robbie's rather fetching nose plaster.

On March 3 Robbie responded to taunts of 'Smackhead' from the Everton fans by simulating cocaine-snorting on the touchline.

And on April 18, Robbie had his nose broken in a lavatorial scuffle in a Liverpool city centre hotel.

Robbie could have been an all-time great. As it is, in the words of Eighties ska band The Specials, he looks in danger of having done too much, much too young. For England's sake we should all hope he gets out of his teens before he is 30.

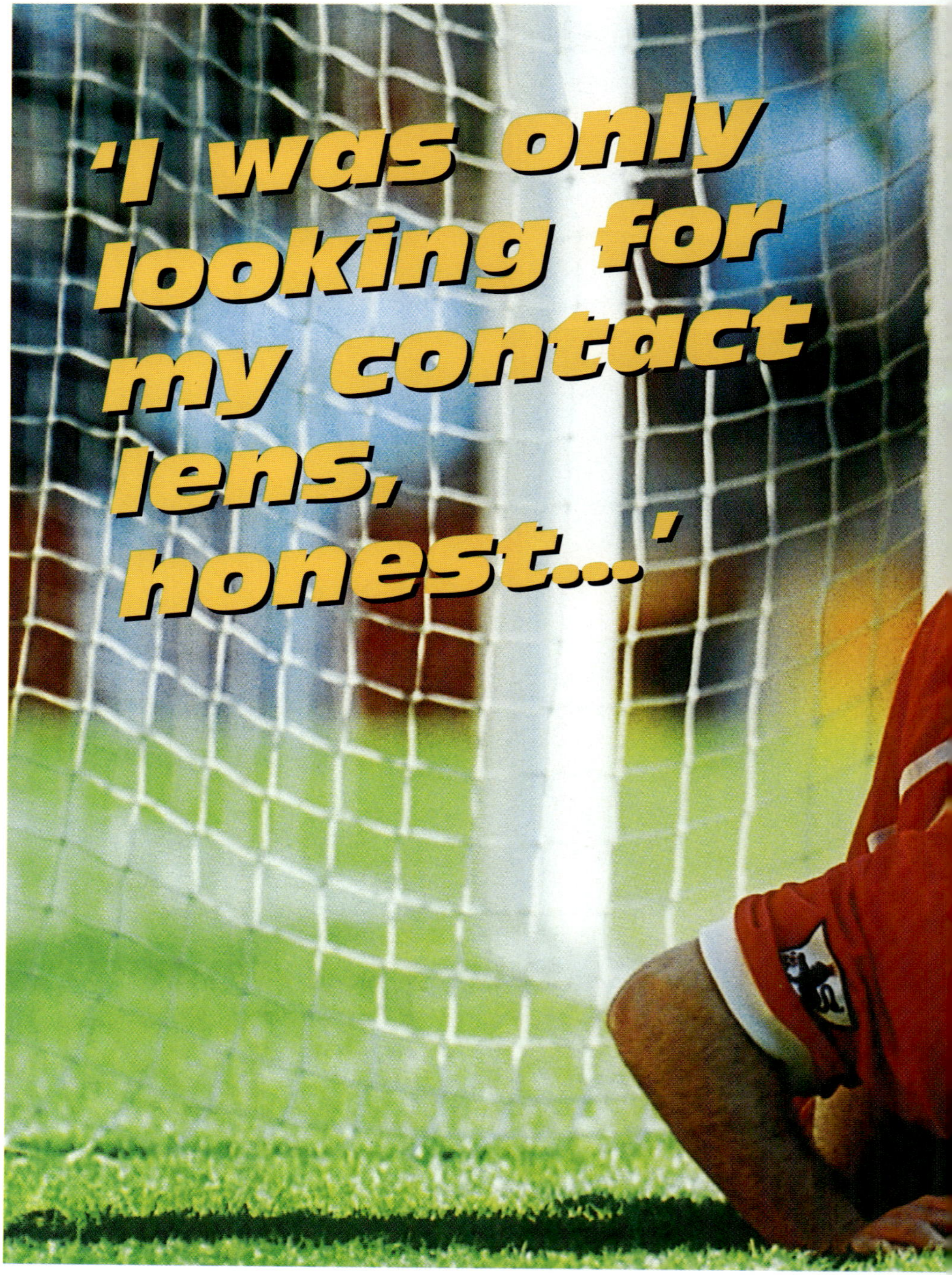

Robbie's goal celebrations... Right: The wrong party line. Above: The striker supports the strikers – at the docks, that is

So that's the reason he wears a plaster on his nose.

HAIRCUT 100 XI

Selecting a Bad Hair XI should be a relatively simple exercise. After all, football has driven some of the worst trends in hairdressing to have afflicted the British Isles in recent years.

Amongst other atrocities we have had the perm, pioneered by Kevin Keegan and adopted by half the British male population; the Greek god brush-forward look, championed by Paul Gascoigne; the blond rinse, which also had the hand of Gascoigne in it; and the pineapple, which thankfully never caught on.

Nevertheless, selecting this XI posed a difficult dilemma. Should we include within the team those players whose barnetary indiscretions were not so much of their own doing, but were more a feature of the era in which they played? If, for example, you were fated to have been 20 years old in 1973, you would have had no choice but to wear your hair long and dress like a clown.

Had you been the same age in the early Eighties you would have had to have a curly (Harry Enfield scouser) perm.

If you were unlucky enough to live in the Eastern bloc in the Seventies or be a member of the Austrian World Cup squad in 1990, you would have looked dreadful on every score.

All of these people – particularly those from the Communist countries – had no say in the matter. Their hairstyles were simply following orders.

So we decided it would be unfair to discriminate against them. Instead, we have used three simple selection criteria:

1. Personal discretion needs to have been a factor in the hairstyle. The player must have used an element of personal choice, maybe even going against the prevailing trend at the time.

2. Deliberately attention-grabbing hairstyles – like Gazza's blond rinse or Vinnie's mohican – are excluded. We see no reason to reward the PR men who concocted these stunts, although we do make an exception for the Pineapple Marketing Board, whose sponsorship of a little-known Nottingham Forest forward was nothing short of genius.

3. We've included in the side as many styles (the word style being used loosely) as we could fit in, ranging from the pudding bowl through the comedy afro to the truly awful. See them and weep.

Haircut 100 XI

Manager
Gerry Francis

Subs bench
Denis Law

Jason's beliefs prevented him from playing on a sundae

PAVEL SRNICEK

The helmet

Pavel, in common with many East Europeans, simply has no idea about style. Or if he has, it is an idea that passed through the West about 30 years ago and has never been heard of since. Pavel sports the pudding-bowl, also known as the helmet. Last seen in England atop Paul McCartney circa 1964. Provides excellent protection in cases of air bombardment.

CARLOS VALDERRAMA

The mop

At first this guy's hairstyle looked like some sick publicity-grabbing stunt. Now, after years with no discernible change, it becomes clear that Valderrama actually likes it like this. It is so awful it almost defies description – it most resembles an upturned mop, or one of those Seventies fibre-optic lamps but with really thick strands. Still, it is truly distinctive – even if it is truly crap.

CHARLIE GEORGE

The girl

One of the most famous sights of the 1970s was Charlie George lying prostrate on the Wembley turf having scored the goal that ultimately clinched the double for Arsenal. If his hairstyle was awful then, it got worse when he moved to Derby. Although receding fast, he elected to leave it long and get it permed. Truly a fashion disaster on every score.

JASON LEE

The pineapple

The biggest talking point of the 1995/96 season for Nottingham Forest fans was Jason Lee's hairstyle of tied-back dreadlocks. Its similarity to a pineapple was noted by Skinner and Baddiel, and visiting fans started singing 'He's got a pineapple on his head' to the tune of the spiritual He's Got The Whole World in His Hands.

The striker's form suffered, and Frank Clark complained about two 'middle-class wide-boys' blighting his striker's career. Lee, transferred in the close season to Watford, took matters into his own hands and had his locks shorn off in July 1996.

ROBERTO BAGGIO

The divine ponytail

Baggio has claimed he is a Buddhist. If he is, then why on earth can't he shave off his hair like most other Buddhists, and save us the pain of having to look at his absurd 'divine ponytail'. It can only have been inspired by

KEVIN KEEGAN – *The curly mullet*
The current England manager can never be completely forgiven for starting one of the worst hair trends of the 20th century – namely, the male perm. A perm looks bad enough on a woman, but on men!! Thanks to Keegan, thousands of men around the country started wearing their hair in this embarrassing manner. Were it not for the fact that Kev so obviously thought the style was good, we might have imagined he was having a laugh at our expense. Still, it provides lots of amusement when looking at photos of your dad.

'Yes, folks, you too can have hair just like mine. Simply keep swigging the great taste of Brut...'

watching *My Little Pony* as a young child. It is, in a word, inexplicable.

MARTIN PETERS
The choirboy
People don't have partings any more – not even schoolboys. Martin Peters, a hero of England's finest hour, still has. When he started out with it, it was not that unusual – but in the last 35 years the parting has practically been outlawed. That hasn't deterred Martin, who has hung on to his steadfastly. You've got to admire him for sticking to his guns, but boy, is it dull.

GEORGE BERRY
The comedy afro
At a time when black players were still fairly thin on the ground, George Berry was one of the path-breakers. A hero at Wolves and Stoke, where the chant 'Ooh Georgie Berry' was a terrace favourite, Berry sported an afro that was so immense it was thought that birds nested in it. Rumour has it that he modelled his style on the Hair Bear Bunch.

DENIS LAW (Sub)
The mongoose
The Lawman was an exceptional footballer within an exceptional United side, and made up the Holy Trinity alongside Charlton and Best. He remains a hero to many who saw him in his pomp – one of whom must have been Rod Stewart, who has modelled his hairstyle on Law's ever since. It was once said that 'he had the reactions of a mongoose and the hairstyle as well'. Denis has stuck by his hairstyle, despite advice to the contrary, for over 30 years.

CLAUDIO CANNIGIA
The piece of string
In his early playing days Claudio had short dark hair, but felt he wasn't getting noticed. So he grew it long and dyed it blond. This worked for a while, earning Cannigia the attention of national team selectors. This wasn't enough for Claudio, who felt he had to go one step further. Hence he pioneered

BARRY VENISON

The mullet

Amazing to think when watching the dapper, short-haired Mr Venison on ITV nowadays, that he was once the nation's standard bearer for the mullet. Barry's version was that of the ageing bleach-blond Costa Brava saddo. His shaggy mane was allied to a dress sense only surpassed in its absence of taste by John Barnes and Mick Skinner.

Ten years on, Barry has finally revealed his magic formula for this hair-do: One bottle of hairspray and two tons of scaffolding

the use of a piece of string in place of a headband. Astonishingly cheap for a man rumoured to blow thousands on cocaine, and astonishingly crap.

GERRY FRANCIS (Manager)

The grey mullet

Gerry Francis seemed quite normal when he was a player. Absolutely dominant in the centre of midfield, he was a man of composure, energy and vision. As a manager he has become quirky and odd – and his hair has taken on a life of its own. Gerry, please do us all a favour and get it cut.

DES WALKER

A slip of the razor

Desmond Walker is not the best-looking of footballers, and perhaps he knows this. He has certainly done everything he can to take attention away from his face by creating a series of hilarious shaven-hair designs. They've looked mainly like the workings of an incompetent DIY enthusiast. Certainly, Des was not looking in the mirror when he concocted them. You'll never beat Des Walker – or emulate his 'tache.

Des Walker: Three lions on his shirt, and two caterpillars on his top lip

KAREL POBORSKY

The mess

Karel Poborsky burst into the British consciousness with his audacious chip over Vitor Baia of Portugal during Euro '96. When he subsequently joined Man Utd, he did little to distinguish himself on the field of play, but he did demonstrate the sartorial awareness associated with most Czechs – i.e. none. At best he looked like he'd been dragged through a hedge backwards, at worst like a dog after falling in a lake and shaking itself dry. But then, any bloke with a bird's name is bound to have a few hang-ups...

Karel got so hungry standing around he decided to eat himself

CHRIS WADDLE

You name it, he's done it

Chris Waddle, like his fellow ex-Newcastle player Mr Venison, now sports a respectable close-cropped hair style. Throughout the Eighties, however, Waddle seemed intent on humiliating himself in public, carrying a series of styles that, had you not known better, you would have assumed he was wearing only for a bet. The worst was the bog-brush at the front, allied to the curly mullet at the rear. A total misjudgement , but it certainly gave us all a laugh. Good on yer, Chris.

The Flying Mullet (left); the Hitler Quiff (right); the Blond Bombshell (below left); the Hedgehog (opposite)

WADDLE
The Hi-Lights

The perm, the mullet, the hedgehog, the ponytail, the helmet, the short back and sides - he's had the lot

The way we wore

The changing styles of the men that other men look up to as role models - from Sixties Brylcreem boys to Nineties Wella Shock Waves wet gel lads

Opposite: England 1966 with the Jules Rimet Trophy for the world's dullest short back 'n' sides
Above: Arsenal 1971, the team that did a unique double – no-style hair and no-style soccer
Below: Man United 1998, the year they won nothing at all ... except Hair Gel Users Of The Year

With the profusion of foreign players in the British game, it's easy to forget that only a few years ago they were very much the exception. All of us of a certain vintage recall those days fondly, not because football in Britain was any better – it certainly wasn't – but because we could make appalling generalisations about foreigners and get away with it.

For example, all players from Europe would find the pace of the British game too fast for them. All South Americans were cheating bastards who our refs would see through in seconds. All Africans – not that we could imagine Africans playing in England – would run for cover as soon as they experienced our 'Arctic' winter conditions. And all Italians were skilful but cowardly and would find our uncompromising defenders too hard for them. Then they actually began to play here...

The best foreign players have proved themselves not only more skilful but also tougher, more resilient and (though this shouldn't surprise us) more intelligent.

The first inroads were made by Muhren and Thijssen, Ardiles and Villa – but the floodgates didn't open until the early Nineties. Since then players such as Cantona, Bergkamp, Schmeichel, Gullit and Petit have changed the course of the British game. But many others haven't.

This XI is a celebration of those who haven't. We rejoice in the instances of highly promising Slavic midfielders who turned out to be work-shy and virulently anti-capitalist; of West Africans who fell ill at the taste of Yorkshire pudding; and of all those players who could only have been bought in cases of mistaken identity – 'Oh, you meant *that* Milosevic.'

We've all had one... This team contains eleven of the best.

ARE YOU SURE THIS IS THE GUY YOU SAW ON THE VIDEO XI

During his days off, Andrea would often be found selling pegs and reading fortunes for local residents

Mr Gross: He had a full head of hair when he started at Spurs

CHRISTIAN GROSS (Manager)

Tottenham manager 1997-8 (above right)
Gross was a gross miscalculation by the Spurs board when looking for a replacement for Mr Mullet, Gerry Francis. He looked good and talked tough on arrival, but it soon became clear he was out of his depth. 'Hapless' was the term most often associated with Gross – when he left White Hart Lane after less than a year, he looked like he had aged about 20 years.

TORBEN PIECHNIK

Liverpool 1992-3, 17 appearances
A Dane, who unusually was an international for Norway, Piechnik was signed as a central defender in 1992. Like the chocolate bar of the same name, Piechnik looked like a lump of shite – and played like one. Although joining a roll call of incompetent Liverpool defenders, Torben stood out as one of the worst.

ANDREA SILENZI

Nottingham Forest 1995-6; 12 appearances, no goals (opposite)
Signed for £1.8m from Torino, Silenzi was one of the first Italians to play in the English league. Having a girl's name wasn't a good start, but what really didn't help was playing like a girl (NB: apologies to Mia Hamm). Abysmally poor in every department of the game, he left after failing to score in any of his 12 sporadic League appearances for Forest.

BRANCO

Middlesbrough 1995-6; 9 appearances
Signed primarily to keep Juninho company, this Brazilian World Cup star arrived in Britain with only one intention – to make as much money as possible with the least amount of effort. About three stone overweight, he had two speeds – slow and slower – and seemed to have left his famed free-kick ability at home in Brazil.

He played only nine League games before Robson tired of him and actually paid him to leave.

FABIO MOREIRA

Middlesbrough 1997; 1 appearance
Fabio Moreira was brought to Middlesbrough solely on the basis that he was Emerson's brother-in-law. An injury crisis in October 1997 meant that his footballing services were called upon. Described in the Footballer's Factfile as 'flashy, with flicks and tricks, but not relishing the tackling side of the game', Fabio clearly learned much from his more celebrated relative.

As he also looked the spitting image of Emerson, he caused great confusion in both the opposition and his own side and only played the one game.

STEPHANE GUIVARC'H

Newcastle 1998; Rangers 1998-9

Something of a mystery, this one. Guivarc'h was top scorer in the French league in the 1997/98 season and played in all of France's World Cup matches. Signed in the close season for £3.5m by Newcastle, he failed to impress and was transferred to Rangers with less than half of the season gone. He has now gone from Rangers as well. We can't recall this happening to Geoff Hurst after 1966.

BERNARD LAMA

West Ham (on loan) 1998, 12 appearances

Lama, a seasoned French international and strong candidate for the Haircut 100 XI, joined West Ham on loan with the avowed intention of playing himself back into the French World Cup side. He did his chances no harm by conceding only six goals in his first eight games, but rather blew it by letting in 15 in the remaining four!! Result – no place back in the French side and end of loan spell.

Bernard did a lot of leaning and pointing during his brief stay at West Ham

Couldn't score in a brothel

ALI DIA

Southampton 1996; 1 substitute appearance

In late 1996 Southampton were going through one of their regular crises. Despite a famous 6-3 win against Man Utd, they were as usual on the fringe of the relegation zone. Imagine Graeme Souness's delight, then, when World Footballer of the Year George Weah phoned up to recommend a player. The player was Ali Dia, a Senegalese international and ex-Paris St Germain striker, available on a free transfer and desperate to play in England.

Souness snapped up Dia and immediately put him into the first team squad for the home game against Leeds. When Matt Le Tissier got injured, Dia was sent on. It became obvious immediately that he was out of his depth. The caller, of course, had not been Weah and the player was an ex-French First Division reserve. Result – one embarrassed Premiership manager and one Senegalese's one and only League appearance.

FLORIN RADUCIOIU

West Ham 1996; 11 appearances, 2 goals

Harry Redknapp's scattergun approach to the purchase of foreign players has led to several high-profile failures. Raducioiu – a massive talent – was perhaps the biggest disappointment. He appeared spectacularly uninterested in playing for East London's finest – even missing a League Cup tie to go shopping at Harvey Nichols! It didn't take long before he returned to Spain, from whence he had so reluctantly come.

NICOLA BERTI (Sub)

Tottenham 1998; 17 appearances, 3 goals

Thirty-eight caps for Italy meant this guy was obviously no joker, but he managed to look out of his depth playing in a very average Spurs side. Another Italian with a girl's first name, he also had an unfortunate cockney rhyming slang surname (Bertie Woofter = … well work it out for yourself). Didn't bode well, and so it proved.

He ran, they ran, everyone ran except Yuran

SERGEI YURAN

Millwall (on loan) 1996; 13 appearances, 1 goal

Yuran – a top Russian international – arrived at Millwall in January 1996 along with his international colleague Vassilli Kulkov. It was supposed to mark a new dawn for Millwall. Instead, the pair didn't train, didn't try and were obviously taking the piss. This is not something any sane person would do in this part of London, but they do say that Moscow is even more dangerous than Millwall these days.

Brolin: a consistent player, consistently crap that is.

TOMAS BROLIN

Leeds 1995-7; Crystal Palace 1998; 32 appearances, 4 goals

It's hard now to believe that Brolin singlehandedly took England apart in the 1992 European Championship. Watching him lumber around the Crystal Palace midfield was like watching Eddie Murphy's fat other half in *The Nutty Professor*. Apparently, when Steve Coppell asked an obviously unfit Brolin to play, Coppell reasoned that 'a wise head can save miles in legs'. Sixteen games and no goals later, the conclusion has to be … sorry, Steve, you were wrong!

JOHN JENSEN

Arsenal 1992-5; 98 appearances, 1 goal

Following Denmark's unexpected triumph in the 1992 European Championships, having a Danish player suddenly became *de rigueur* at Europe's top clubs. Jensen flattered to deceive with his goal in the Euro Final – he famously scored only one for Arsenal in his entire four-year stay.

'It's true! Wearing a tall hat does make your nose look smaller'

I DON'T FANCY YOURS MUCH XI

It's said that beauty is in the eye of the beholder, but ugly mugs are something that everyone seems to agree upon. Take the star performer in this team – Peter Beardsley.

Super personality he may be (and how often have we used that phrase when describing less than attractive women?) Magnificent player and ambassador for the game he most certainly is. But even his wife would admit that Beardo is no oil painting (unless you count the works of Francis Bacon, of course).

The same is true for most of the selections in this team.

Looking like Frankenstein's monster is not technically a disadvantage in football. However, to have made it to the top of the profession as an 'ugly' probably required more guts and determination than your better-looking colleagues.

For a start you were probably picked last in schoolyard games among your mates. This will have had nothing to do with how good you really were, but will have been determined by the subconscious association that most boys make between looks and ability.

There may be something Darwinian in this, as prehistoric men came to the same realisation that most of us have reached in our lives – that our best chance of getting a shag was hanging around with the best-looking bloke in the hope of picking up his cast-offs.

On the pitch itself you were doubtless singled out by the opposition for rough verbal treatment. Nowadays there are laws against racism and sexism, but no one has yet thought to clamp down on the widespread practice of face-ism.

Many players delight in marshalling their defence with words along the lines of 'Steve, you take the centre-forward, Bill you take the winger and John, you mark the ugly one.'

If you can get this in early and thereafter develop your play as a team (all team-mates have to join in and embellish the descriptions as the game goes on), it can really demoralise an opponent.

So it's not easy, and these men deserve our admiration. Admire on.

Manager:
Frank Clark

Subs bench
Gianfranco Zola
Iain Dowie

Iain Dowie: Hoping for a spot up front alongside Ronaldo

STEVE OGRIZOVIC

Lurch from The Addams Family

'Oggy' Ogrizovic started his career in league football in 1977. In the 22 years since, he has been frightening opposing attackers, and sometimes his own defenders, simply by looking at them. His already lugubrious face has lengthened over these years, and now measures over 18 inches from top to bottom.

PHILIP NEVILLE

Herman Munster's love child

Philip Neville is the member of the Man United side least likely to be offered a modelling contract. If Becks is a character out of Jane Austen, Neville is a character out of Dickens. The poor chap looks as if his face was pressed very hard from both sides when he was a wee lad, resulting in his now unnaturally long and thin visage.

MARTIN KEOWN

A man called Horse

The Arsenal defender's ability to track and stick to his prey for 90 minutes and longer must surely indicate the presence of animal blood within him. His tracking skills would suggest he is part dog, but his looks imply horse. So half dog, half horse – what a combination.

PHIL THOMPSON (Opposite)

Concorde

Phil Thompson and Ray Clemence, despite playing together in the same all-conquering Liverpool side for years, were not allowed within six feet of each other on the pitch for fear their noses would collide, rendering one or other unconscious. Centre-back Thompson's conk was truly magnificent, measuring six inches from base to apex. That's C-O-N-K, conk.

COLIN HENDRY

Raging albino

Hendry is the archetypal terrifying Scotsman – he would have been a natural for a role in *Braveheart*. With his bright red, craggy face and that absurdly blond straggly mane, his 'Och-aye-the-noo ye f*ckin' Sassenach' looks imply that he is a relic from a bygone age. Probably the ice age!

MATT LE TISSIER

Gormless nark

If Matthew Le Tissier is Le God, as so many Southampton fans believe, thank Le God for not making us all in his own image. His extensive schnozz sits atop a drooping mouth, thus creating one of the dopiest expressions in British football. It has long been said that there is too much interbreeding on Guernsey, but we can't comment on that.

Don't Fancy Yours Much XI

RONALDO
Plug from The Bash Street Kids

The world's finest footballer sadly does not have looks to match his talent. He has little going for him in the facial department and has a mouth and teeth that would not look out of place on a donkey. Doesn't stop him going out with a stunning blonde, however. What can it be that she sees in him?

GIANFRANCO ZOLA (Sub)
Droopy

Gianfranco Zola has one of those faces in which five or six things seem to be moving all at once. The Chelsea playmaker is such a lovely fella, you can't help warming to him. But Italy's little genius does look like his ancestors missed a couple of stages of human evolution. Vaguely prehistoric.

And you thought all Italians looked like Al Pacino...

ANDY HINCHCLIFFE
Jimmy Hill's love child

Aside from Jimmy Hill and David Coulthard, Andy Hinchcliffe possesses the biggest chin in British sport. Rumours abound that his jaw has been specially strengthened to enable him to lift the chin when eating.

NOBBY STILES
Dirty old man

Bald, toothless and chinless is no way to go through life, Norbert. Nobby Stiles was the pin-up for geriatrics throughout Britain in 1966. They saw him as one of their own despite him being only 24.

IAIN DOWIE (sub)
Gruesome

Iain Dowie's permanently pained expression may reflect his 110 per cent, never-say-die attitude – or, more likely, constipation. Dowie has led several lines with little distinction, although you can't fault him for effort.

FRANK CLARK (Manager)
Mutant

Many players go badly off when they stop playing. Frank Clark was off to start with. He was famously likened to Mr Potato Head. Mr Potato Head should sue.

JAAP STAM
Zombie

In a previous life, Stam may well have been used as a model for the Easter Island stone statues. Whether true or not, Stam's skeletal look speaks of one who has only recently been raised from the dead. Spooky.

Winner best nickname category: Crap Stam

PETER BEARDSLEY

Quasimodo

Peter Beardsley is one of the most widely respected footballers in the UK. He played in the great Liverpool side of the late Eighties, the nearly-great Newcastle side of the mid-Nineties and the ... well, rather average Everton side in between. He was the ideal partner for Rush, Aldridge, Lineker and Andy Cole and managed to score a goal every three games in his own right.

He has been a gentleman throughout his career, and is clearly a man who loves the game like a fan – so much so that he turned out for lowly Hartlepool for most of the 1998/99 season.

He is also, truth be told, one of the least attractive specimens at large in the UK. It's not his fault – his raw materials were obviously not great and on top of these he has suffered at least two broken cheekbones – but it's still undeniable.

Beardsley looks and sounds like a man a couple of sandwiches short of the full picnic. Still Peter, we love you and salute you – you are an inspiration.

'Attention, Earthlings! When my fellow Beardsleys from the Planet Beardsley conquer your puny Earth, all men will wish to look like me! Ah-ha-ha-haaa!'

Bruce Grobbelaar: Still hanging on to to his old junior school kitbag

Jan Molby: Fourteen stones and rising

Gary Gillespie: Not bad-looking ... didn't last long at Anfield

Kenny Dalglish: Unintelligible and unprepossessing

Alan Kennedy: Nicknamed Horse, and it wasn't because of his speed on the flat

Phil Neal: How did this man win 50 caps for England?

Is this the ugliest team of all time?

1984. European champions Liverpool reveal the line-up they are sending to face Independiente in the World Club Championship. Having frightened the wits out of all those namby-pamby Latins in Europe, they thought their best tactic was to put out the most gruesome-looking squad ever assembled in the hope that Independiente would run screaming back to South America. But their wily opponents turned up wearing blindfolds and thus won 1-0.

Alan: Before he was Hansen

Ian Rush: The speed of a greyhound, the face of a whippet

Craig Johnstone: Modelled Emerson's hair before Emerson

John Wark: Body chiselled out of granite, face modelled out of Play-Doh

Steve Nicol: Still playing, still scary

WHO'S A PRETTY BOY THEN XI

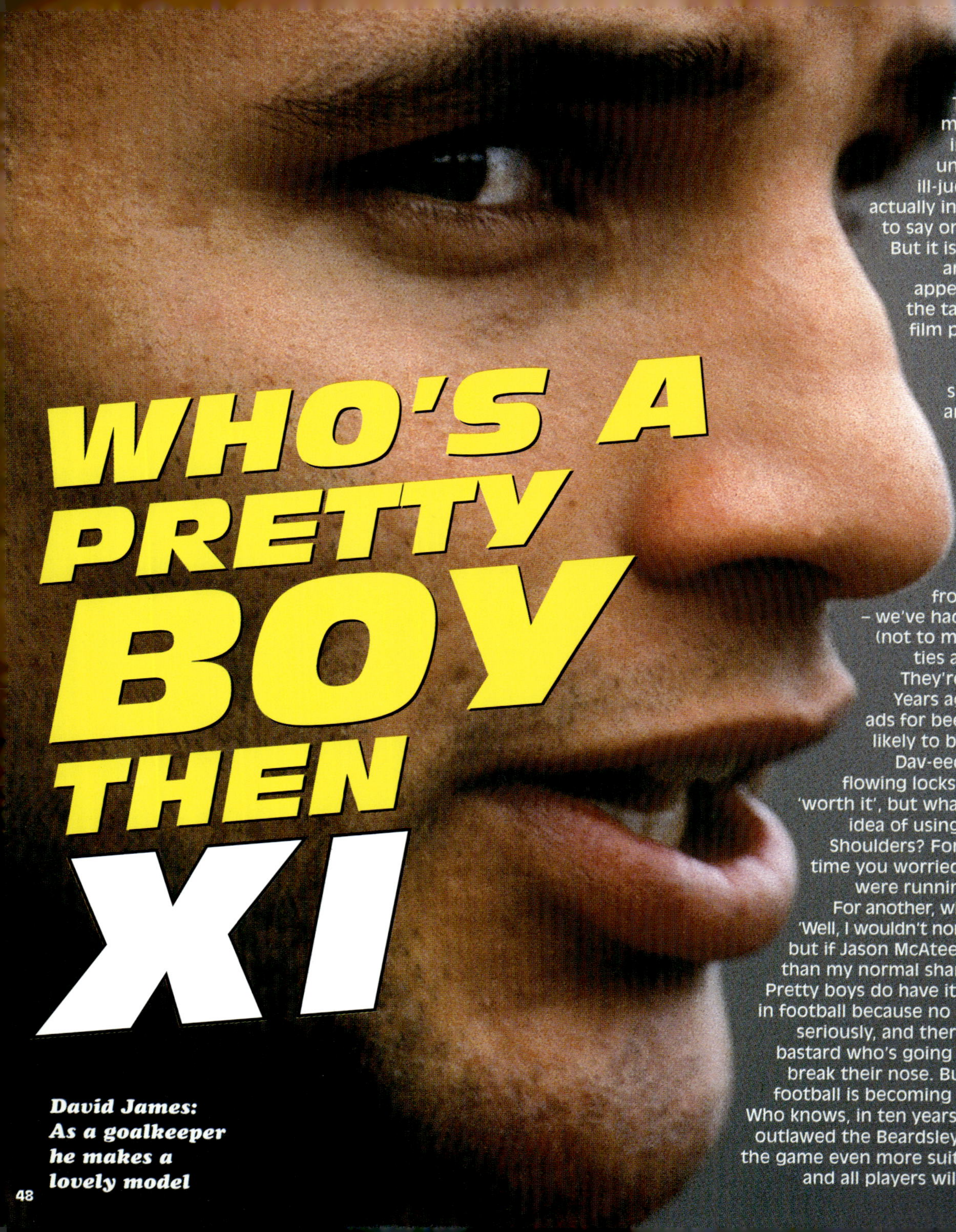

David James: As a goalkeeper he makes a lovely model

They say that footballers are the new rock stars. They certainly demonstrate many of the characteristics – insane drinking sessions, an unstoppable sex drive and an ill-judged belief that people are actually interested in what they have to say on topics outside of football. But it is more true that footballers are the new soap stars. They appear in the 'news' sections of the tabloids, turn up at the right film premieres and get paid vast sums to do things they are really no good at – such as singing, hosting chat shows and, increasingly, modelling. There is a growing list of footballers who have made money from modelling – David James, Gary Speed and Trevor Sinclair to name but three. And it's no longer just football gear and clothes from Top Man that they sport – we've had them in posh dress shirts (not to mention Posh's dress skirts), ties and, worryingly, spectacles. They're even plugging cosmetics. Years ago, footballers appeared in ads for beer and fags – now it's more likely to be skin toner and shampoo. Dav-eed Ginola, with his gorgeous flowing locks and gallic charm, is clearly 'worth it', but what genius came up with the idea of using Jason McAteer for Head & Shoulders? For a start, when was the last time you worried about dandruff while you were running around a football pitch? For another, when have you ever thought, 'Well, I wouldn't normally use Head & Shoulders but if Jason McAteer uses it, it must be better than my normal shampoo.' Never, that's when. Pretty boys do have it a little harder than others in football because no one ever really takes them seriously, and there's always some hard, ugly bastard who's going to make a special effort to break their nose. But things are changing and football is becoming more equal opportunities. Who knows, in ten years' time they may even have outlawed the Beardsleys and Southgates to make the game even more suitable for the TV audience – and all players will have to be good-looking.

Subs bench
Dean Holdsworth
Patrik Berger
Jamie Redknapp

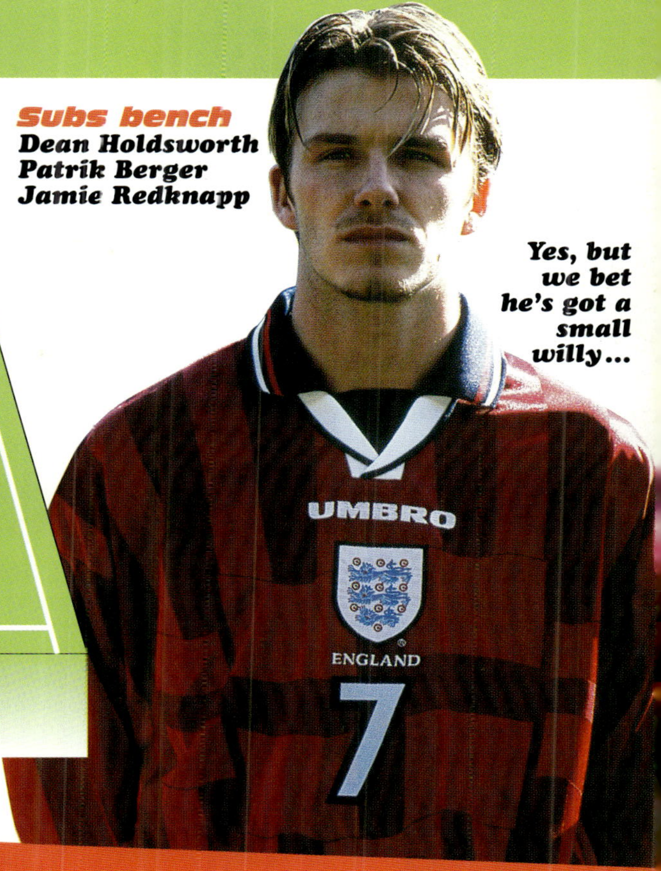

Yes, but we bet he's got a small willy…

DAVID JAMES

David James has done more modelling than most other footballers. Standing 6'5" in his stockinged feet and possessed of rugged good looks, he is frequently in demand … which is more than you can say for his footballing skills.
Key target audience: Saturday night party girls 18-25

GRAEME LE SAUX

Graeme Le Saux has the sort of little-boy-lost looks that make it even more surprising when he starts fighting with his own team-mates – such as the famous bust-up with David Batty – or tangling with nasty, insulting opponents like that horrid Robbie Fowler. An intelligent, good-natured lad off the pitch, renowned for having read a book, Graeme does have a tendency to become 'animated' on it.
Key target audience: Um…

DAVID BECKHAM

Now one half of the world's most glamorous couple, the man voted Europe's Most Valuable Player – and no doubt Europe's most shaggable, too, as far as the teen mags are concerned – David looks set to continue his reign as fantasy date for the pre-pubescent. Despite absurd facial hair arrangements, retains boyish good looks.
Key target audience: Girls 8-14.

JAMIE REDKNAPP (Sub)

Redknapp is a poor girl's Beckham. Not quite as pretty, not quite as talented and married to someone not quite as rich (pop singer Louise). Still, he does have a certain appeal. And he does provide the amusing prospect that his looks will go off and he will end up looking like his dad!!
Consolation for all of us.
Key target audience: Aspiring pop singers.

EMMANUEL PETIT

Despite wearing his hair in a ponytail, Monsieur Petit manages to look hard and manly at the same time as being sensitive and in touch with his feminine side. Many think he should have been player of the season in England in the 1998/9 season – and he scored a goal IN THE WORLD CUP FINAL !! Magnifique.
Key target audience: University graduates, 25-35.

ALLY McCOIST

Wee Ally McCoist is such a jocular, matey chap, it's hard to remember he is one of the leading all-time goalscorers in British football. His cheeky grin and boyish charm make him the housewives' favourite, even if none of them know he plays for Kilmarnock.
Key target audience: Mums with kids 30-45.

LES FERDINAND

When he was dating Dani Behr, Newcastle fans delighted in chanting 'He's here, he's there, he's shagging Dani Behr, Ferdinand, Ferdinand'. Sir Les was rumoured to be a bit of a swordsman during his time at the Magpies, but it didn't affect his football. He was still crap.
Key target audience: Anything that moves.

Les's proudest moment was modelling for the Saga magazine woollens catalogue

The Czech national team were so short of cash they had to ration the razors

JOHN SCALES

In a previous era John Scales would have been a Grenadier Guardsman. Upright, respectable, capable of standing in the same place for hours on end – not dissimilar to his footballing style. Possesses classically British old-fashioned charm.
Key target audience: The better-heeled woman.

SOL CAMPBELL

Sol commands respect. A top performer on the pitch, he is shaping into a useful captain and seems a nice, intelligent boy besides. He looks as if he's chiselled out of marble and really is a magnificent physical specimen.
Key target audience: All women who are not lesbian – and some who are.

RYAN GIGGS

Ryan Giggs has been supplanted by Becks in the affections of the nation's under-age girlies. But he retains a strong fan base among those who 'grew up' with him on their walls. Bare-shirted celebration vs Arsenal remains highlight of season for much of UK's female population.
Key target audience: Developing girls 14-20.

WARREN BARTON

One of those players who looked good at Wimbledon but crap anywhere else. Mystifyingly selected for England not once but three times, Warren really is quite pretty.
Key target audience: Frustrated housewifes, 25-40

PATRIK BERGER (Sub)

Berger is a rarity – a Czech without a mullet. He does, of course, have long hair, although it is styled à la Ginola to flow majestically behind him. Patrick is a sensitive lad who needs confidence to play at his best. We know several young ladies who would happily provide him with more confidence.
Key target audience: Students 18-25.

Dean: More scores on page three than on the back page

DEAN HOLDSWORTH (Sub)

One can excuse Mr Holdsworth's well-documented indiscretions, as he really is quite a handsome dog. Dark and rugged in the continental manner, it is something of a disappointment to find that he comes from Walthamstow. Added appeal comes in the form of an identical twin who looks quite a lot like him.
Key target audience: Page 3 stunnas

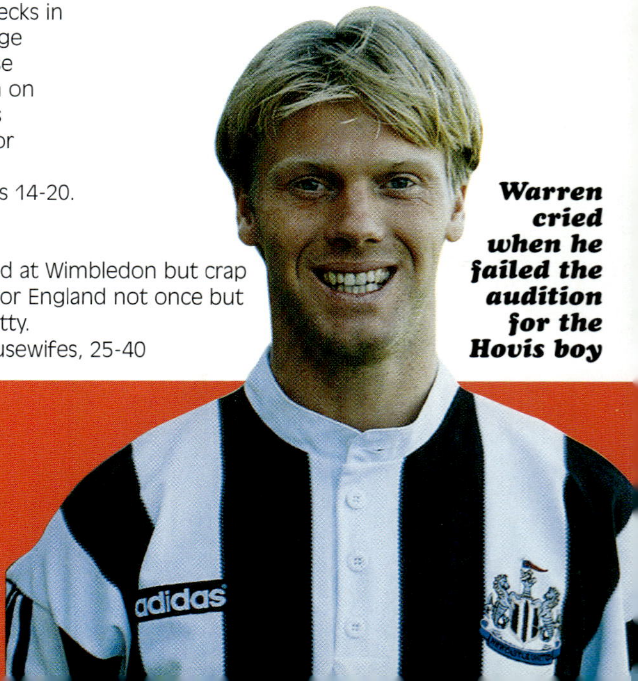

Warren cried when he failed the audition for the Hovis boy

DAVID GINOLA

'I am not a movie star, I am a footballer.' Maybe, but Ginola is the closest thing football has to a movie star. He played like a god in 1998/99 and looked like one as well. He was also unbelievably French. The shrugs, the pouts, the staged emotional outbursts when denied yet another dubious penalty, the charm and the Gallic mystery. He has it all ... oh, and the hair as well. We think you're worth it Dav-eed. **Key target audience:** Women with split ends.

David picking up one of his two awards for best-kept hair in the 1998/99 season

STAR PLAYER PROFILE

Teams: Toulon, Racing Paris, Brest, Paris St Germain, Newcastle, Spurs. League games 122; Goals 15; Caps 17.

HARD XI

As with most sports, football has its fair share of old codgers who insist that the game was far better in the Forties, Fifties, Sixties or Seventies. (Strangely, the only people who reckon the game was better in the Eighties are Liverpudlians). These claims mystify those of us who look at old footage with a fresh eye and laugh at the slow pace of the game, the poor pitches, the inept goalkeeping and the apparent lack of any tactics.

The one claim that does appear to have substance is that the game was harder in the past. Or if not harder, then certainly dirtier. Watching videos of games from the early Seventies is a little like watching *Dr Who* when you were a kid – you have to hide behind the sofa at the scary bits.

You see tackles at shin height, from behind, two-footed – even three-footed – and in most cases the whistle isn't even blown. To get booked you had to break an opponent's bone, to get sent off you had to commit manslaughter.

There are many reasons why the game was harder in the past. Rules on what constituted a foul were less restrictive, fewer games were televised so a dirty player could get away with it for longer, and defenders had none of these fancy modern pretensions about being able to play proper football.

They just wanted to boot the ball and their opponent into the stands.

But, one basic truth underpins all of this: players and people were tougher than they are today. They came from tougher stock, they were brought up tougher and they stayed tougher. Just look at some of them. Ron 'Chopper' Harris – more than 700 League games for Chelsea and Brentford; Norman 'Bites Yer Legs' Hunter – over 650 League games; and Jack 'I've Got a Little List' Charlton – more than 600 League games, all for Leeds. Players today have neither the nicknames nor the staying power.

So, players of yesteryear were almost certainly harder and they make up most of this team. Some of the tougher modern players also make it, largely because we're scared of them and they can still run fast. So read on, and in the words of the best horror movies – be afraid, be very afraid!

Tommy Smith: The Ironman (no, he didn't work in a laundry)

Subs bench
Steve McMahon
Vinnie Jones
Billy Bremner

Roy Keane: A pussycat really

TOMMY 'IRONMAN' SMITH

One of the saddest sights in recent years has been Tommy Smith hobbling around on two legs that, after years of punishment, are barely able to support the rest of his body. Some of Smith's former opponents might say this is justice for the abuse his tackles inflicted, but most will be sympathetic. Smith was hard but rarely dirty – he simply put everything he had into getting the ball off the opposition. An Anfield legend.
Best quote: 'Tommy Smith could start a riot in a graveyard.' – Bill Shankly

RON 'CHOPPER' HARRIS

Chelsea during the late Sixties and Seventies were a curious breed of the sublime and the not so sublime. Providing the platform for performers like Hudson and Osgood was a tough, sometimes nasty defence anchored for almost 20 years by the dapper Mr Harris. Harris was a mere 5'7" but was capable of intimidating almost anyone, as was shown in the 1970 FA Cup Final, when Chelsea, led by Harris, 'out-harded' the famously hard Leeds side.
Best quote: 'If Harris was in a good mood he'd put iodine on his studs before a game.' – Jimmy Greaves

NORMAN 'BITES YER LEGS' HUNTER

Many people remember Norman Hunter for his famous non-tackle of Poland's Lato in the ultimately disastrous World Cup qualifier in 1973. People recall it so vividly not so much because of the awful consequences – failure to qualify for the finals – but more because it was so uncharacteristic of Hunter, probably the strongest tackler the game has seen.
Best moment: Unprovoked attack on Franny Lee in 1975 that led to one of the finest bouts of fisticuffs ever seen on an English football field.
Best quote: 'Norman Hunter doesn't tackle opponents so much as break them down for resale as scrap.' – Julie Welch

ROY 'KEANO' KEANE

Roy Keane has attempted to soften his public image throughout the late 1990s. There has been much talk about the moderating effect of kids and marriage and of the maturity that comes with age. And then ... he goes and spoils it all with an act of random violence on the pitch that leads to yet another yellow or red card. Keano is a hard lad who brooks no cheek either on or off the pitch. Not to be messed with.

Members of the public beware

MICK HARFORD

The initiation ritual at Wimbledon has traditionally involved having your clothes sliced up then you being dumped naked in a public place. Strangely, this ritual was not enacted on Mick Harford, whose reputation for being a hard case saw him exempted by the Crazy Gang. Harford was not a man to be trifled with either on or off the pitch.
Best moment: The 1987 night when Harford and Tony Coton laid out six roadworkers in a Hemel Hempstead pub, leaving two requiring hospital treatment.

'Did someone say I was soft?'

STEVE 'THE ENFORCER' McMAHON (Sub)

Steve McMahon is the player who has been missing from the Liverpool line-up ever since he moved on to Man City in 1991 – the midfield enforcer. McMahon was never one not to get his retaliation in first. If someone managed to stick one on him first – as Vinnie Jones did in 1988 – McMahon would generally be seen chasing them down through the entire game and not stopping until he had 'righted the wrong'.

JACK 'I'VE GOT A LITTLE LIST' CHARLTON

Jack Charlton was uncompromising as a manager and uncompromising as a player. He probably doesn't give bugger-all away when playing snap. For over 600 matches for Leeds he gave nothing away without making his opponents fight bloody hard for it. His famous comments about his 'little list' (of players from whom he was going to extract retribution for previous indiscretions) were much exaggerated by the press, but knowing Jack they probably weren't far from the truth.

STUART 'PSYCHO' PEARCE

Off the pitch, with his quiet voice and apologetic demeanour, Stuart Pearce looks as though butter wouldn't melt. On it he becomes a different animal, pumped up to the max and prepared to eat his opponents, never mind tackle them.
Best moment: Not his insane ecstasy after converting the penalty vs Spain in Euro '96, but his reaction after his stunning free kick in the 1991 FA Cup Final – no reaction, just a blank killer expression. True madness.

VINNIE 'DE NIRO' JONES (Sub)

By no stretch of the imagination is Vincent Jones a skilful footballer. Nonetheless the former hod-carrier has built a career of some distinction on intimidation and hard tackling. His successful venture into films saw him star as a ruthless hit man, a role he has performed on the field for years.
Best moment: Smashing a fellow gangster's head in a sunbed in ***Lock, Stock and Two Smoking Barrels.***

GRAEME 'MY OWN GREATEST FAN' SOUNESS

Graham Souness was one of the great enigmas of modern football – a player of great skill and vision capable of opening up a game with a single pass whilst at the same time a player of great violence capable of opening up an opponent's leg with a single well-timed knee-high challenge.
Worst moment: Tackle on Hibs' George McCluskey that left McCluskey needing nine stitches in a knee wound.

'It shoulda been me in Octopussy'

JOE 'JAWS' JORDAN

Joe Jordan's toothless grin became a regular feature of the League circuit – usually after the muscular Scot had buried the ball in the back of the net. He led the line at Leeds and Manchester United for ten years and gained 52 caps for Scotland. His lack of teeth added menace to his natural aggression and energy, and he often put his head in where feet feared to tread.
Best moment: Making his arm look Welsh when handling the ball in the area to draw the penalty that took Scotland to the 1978 World Cup Finals.

BERT 'NECK' TRAUTMANN

Bert Trautmann can lay claim to being not only one of the hardest footballers of all time, but one of the hardest men, period. Trautmann, playing for Man City against Birmingham in the 1956 FA Cup Final and with 17 minutes to go, dived at the feet of Birmingham's Murphy and broke his neck. Having regained consciousness, he then played the rest of the game!!

Trautmann had already been through a lot. In the war he had joined the Luftwaffe's parachute regiment. During his service he was court-martialled and imprisoned by his own side, was captured by and escaped from both the Russians and the French resistance, had a hand grenade blow up in his face and, finally, was captured by the British.

He was one of only 90 from an original 1,000 of the regiment to survive the war. It was while he was a PoW in England that he began to keep goal.

Trautmann's broken neck was not actually diagnosed for a few days, during which time he was treated by an osteopath (ouch!) His operation to repair the damage involved having holes drilled into his skull to allow a caliper to hold his head in place, and his head and back were in plaster and metal for weeks. Despite all of this he was back in the first team just seven months after the accident. Some man.

DAVE 'TIGER' MACKAY

Dave Mackay was one of the most effective midfielders in Britain in the 1960s. Skilful, visionary, a great leader and a very, very hard player, Mackay was a colossus who brought success to every team he played for.

Best moment: His famous contretemps with the also-not-soft Billy Bremner, demonstrating the eerily powerful presence of this man.

BILLY 'RED' BREMNER

(Sub)

Billy Bremner was one of the most effective midfielders in Britain in the early 1970s. Skilful, visionary, a great leader and a very, very hard player, Bremner was a classic hot-headed redhead who was never far from trouble either on or off the pitch.

Best moment: His famous contretemps with Dave Mackay, who was among the former adversaries – including Nobby Stiles – who said farewell to Bremner at his funeral in 1997.

Hands up if you think you're the HARDEST TEAM OF ALL TIME

Leeds United in the early Seventies were both skilful and brutal. This picture shows the team they put out against Queen's Park Rangers on April 27, 1974. They were a rum lot...

1 **DAVID HARVEY** – Farmer who once withdrew from an international as two of his cows were giving birth.

2 **PAUL REANEY** – Chimp-like full-back. Motto: 'Thou shalt not pass.'

3 **TREVOR CHERRY** – Solid, fair, good at his job. A dull cove for this team.

4 **BILLY BREMNER** – Pound for pound there has never been anyone more competitive.

5 **GORDON McQUEEN** – Pouty lips, blond hair and suggestive surname belied his tough-tackling persona.

6 **NORMAN HUNTER** – Legendary hard man famed for great scrap with Franny Lee.

7 **PETER LORIMER** – The hardest shot in football.

8 **ALLAN CLARKE** – Sniffer's boot was never that far from the keeper's nuts.

9 **JOE JORDAN** – Jaws went in where angels feared to tread.

10 **JOHN GILES** – Great skill but also a great stirrer who 'started' the Keegan-Bremner Charity Shield spat.

11 **PAUL MADELEY** – Made millions from DIY. (Er...)

Sub: **TERRY YORATH** – Managed Wales. Is anything tougher?

Manager: **DON REVIE** – Mad, bad, dangerous to know. Genius.

GLOVERAL

The worst players ever to play for ENGLAND XI

Overhead kick – Warning: Do not attempt this if you are totally lacking in talent

After years in denial, many of us are now coming to the conclusion that the rest of the world reached some time ago. Namely that England are crap at football.

Yes, we have a proud history. We were unbeaten at home from 1872 to 1953, we won the World Cup in 1966 and we even beat Sweden once, though no one can remember when. We've also had our high spots – putting one over the Dutch at Euro '96 was sweetness itself, and Platty's overhead against Belgium was unexpectedly god-like.

However, on balance we've been resolutely mediocre. We haven't beaten Germany since 1985, Norway since 1980, Romania since 1970 and, for the record, the last time we beat Sweden was 1968. Our recent trophy record reads a little like Middlesbrough's – Tournoi de France Winners 1997 and, erm, World Cup Fair Play Award 1998, and that was only jointly with the French.

In the circumstances, finding names for a team of the worst players to have played for England was not difficult. The hard part was whittling down the vast array of candidates. There are the dark years of the mid-Seventies when, despite our clubs winning most of the European club competitions, we were unable to qualify for two successive World Cups. There are the early Eighties when a string of outstandingly ordinary players were selected by Bobby Robson. And, of course, there are the Taylor years – of which more below.

There are, in fact, so many players to choose from that we've had to set some pretty stringent selection criteria.

First, we have not selected any one-cap wonders. Sadly this freezes out of the squad such luminaries as Jason Wilcox, Brian Stein of Luton, Andy Gray of Crystal Palace, Trevor Whymark, Jimmy Rimmer, Neil Ruddock and the excellently named S. R. Bastard (one appearance in a losing side in 1880).

Second, we have dropped all those who gained caps only in the 'joke' Australian tours of 1980 and 1983. This puts paid to the likes of Nigel Spink, Nick Pickering of Sunderland, Alan Sunderland not of Sunderland, Mark Barham and Peter Ward of Brighton. Don't be surprised if you've never heard of these guys. Subsequent England managers didn't seem to have heard of them either.

Finally, we have tried to avoid acting out of malice. The temptation to select Emlyn Hughes was great, but we held back. Hating someone is no reason to include them. This England XI is plain bad.

Subs bench
Paul Mariner

The ball's behind you, Graham

PETER BONETTI

7 caps, 1966-1970

Unlucky to play at the same time as the deity that was Gordon Banks, Peter Bonetti was actually a pretty decent keeper who conceded only one goal in his first six internationals. His performance in his seventh (and last), however, condemns him to eternal life in England's Hall of Shame.

Called into the 1970 World Cup quarter-final side to replace Banks, who had suffered a mystery stomach bug, Bonetti saw his side go 2-0 up against West Germany. Three goalkeeping errors later and probably the best post-war England side were on their way back home. Unforgivable.

LUTHER BLISSETT (opposite)

14 caps, 1983-84, 3 goals

More than a few heads were turned in 1984 when Luther Blissett was signed by AC Milan from Watford. Milan were not then the powerhouse that they are today, but still, here was one of the world's biggest clubs coming in for a player whose first touch often put the ball into another postcode. Rumour has it they meant to sign his team-mate John Barnes, but got the wrong man!

Blissett did actually score a hat-trick for England ... although it was against Luxembourg. Fortunate.

STEVE FOSTER

3 caps, 1982, no goals

Hard to believe now, but Brighton and Hove Albion were once a pretty good side. In the top division for four seasons in the early Eighties, they also reached the FA Cup Final before Smith missed and the wheels well and truly came off. At the heart of their defence stood the gutsy Steve Foster, who came to attention mainly for his use of an absurd Bjorn Borg headband. He somehow made it into the England squad and played in a World Cup game no less, but was soon found out for the limited trier that he was.

GRAHAM ROBERTS (above)

6 caps, 1983-84, no goals

A controversial choice, as Roberts remains a hero to many Spurs fans who yearn for his robust presence in their lightweight midfield. Roberts, however, was little more than an early Vinnie Jones, making up for his technical deficiencies with hard work and hard tackling. Roberts came from non-League football and looked like it. Agricultural.

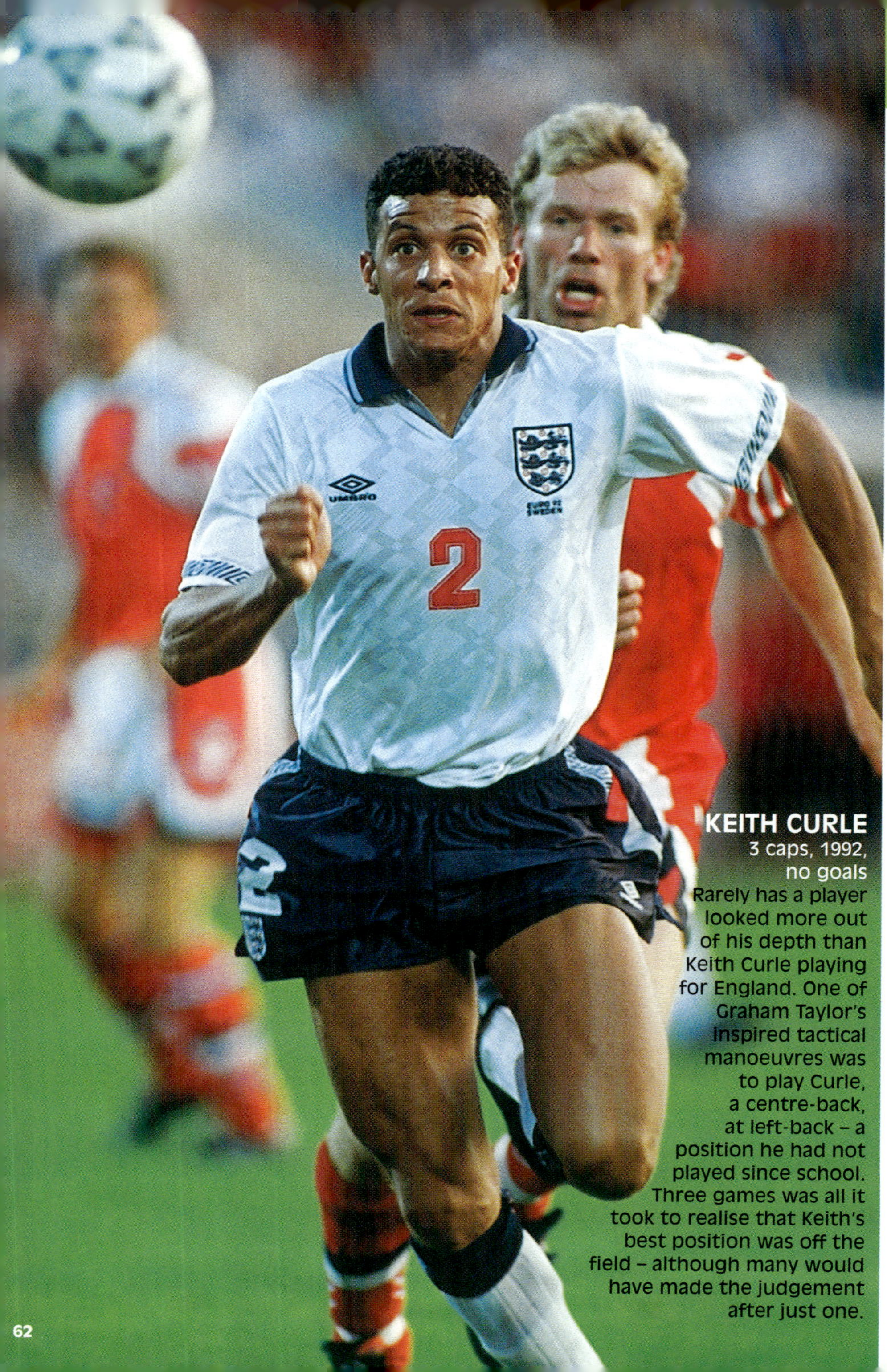

KEITH CURLE

3 caps, 1992, no goals

Rarely has a player looked more out of his depth than Keith Curle playing for England. One of Graham Taylor's inspired tactical manoeuvres was to play Curle, a centre-back, at left-back – a position he had not played since school. Three games was all it took to realise that Keith's best position was off the field – although many would have made the judgement after just one.

TERRY FENWICK

20 caps, 1984-88, no goals

Terry Fenwick earns his place in this side on the basis of one incident in one match – the 1986 World Cup quarter-final vs Argentina. Already 1-0 up due to 'the hand of God', Maradona embarks on an incredible run from the halfway line. Coming towards the England box he approaches Fenwick, the acknowledged axeman of the England team. All of England awaits the cynical foul. Instead, Fenwick moves aside and waves Maradona through. Two seconds later, goal, and England 2-0 down. Inexplicable.

RAY 'BUTCH' WILKINS

84 caps, 1976-87, 3 goals

OK, so Butch was a pretty useful player, but he never did anything much good for his country. A dynamic attacking midfielder at the start of his career, he seemed to regress almost as quickly as his hairline, and became known as the crab for his sideways movement whenever he put on an England shirt. And he was the first Englishman to get sent off in a World Cup match. Slaphead.

JOHN BARNES

79 caps, 1983-96, 11 goals

John Barnes was the star player for England throughout the late-1980s – the man whose exquisite skill and ability to do the impossible would dig us out of unwinnable positions and turn us into worldbeaters. Only he never did. Except for once, in a meaningless friendly in Brazil. Sorry, John, you weren't that bad, but you let us down too often.

JOHN FASHANU

2 caps, 1989, no goals

Decent TV presenter, successful entrepreneur, expert in martial arts, gambler with surprising winning record!! – John Fashanu has many talents. Unfortunately, scoring in an England shirt isn't one of them. Fash was brought into the England side during a goal-scoring famine, and did nothing to indicate that he could alleviate it. Made Steve Bull look international class – which did some doing. Out of his depth.

Worst Players Ever To Play For England XI

PAUL MARINER

35 caps, 1977-85, 13 goals

By any normal standards, Paul Mariner's record makes him too good to place in England's Worst XI. He had a good scoring record, worked hard for the team and was key to England getting into the 1982 World Cup Finals after two previous failures. There was just something about him. Perhaps it was the effete goal celebrations or the atrocious hairstyle. Most probably it was the shorts – tighter than cycling shorts and smaller than Y-fronts. Unpardonable.

To cheer us all up (apart from the Scots, Welsh and Irish)

ENGLAND'S 10 BEST WINS

1. **England 4 West Germany 2 (aet)** World Cup Final 1966
2. **England 4 Holland 1** European Championship 1996
3. **Portugal 0 England 10** Friendly 1947
4. **England 3 Italy 2** Friendly 1934
5. **Germany 3 England 6** Friendly 1938
6. **England 9 Scotland 3** Home International 1961
7. **France 1 England 3** World Cup 1st Round 1982
8. **Spain 2 England 4** Friendly 1987
9. **England 5 Scotland 1** Home International 1975
10. **Ireland 0 England 13** Home International 1882

Couldn't hit barn door

GEOFF THOMAS

9 caps, 1991-2, no goals

A workmanlike midfielder whose ship came in when he was selected by Graham Taylor in 1991. Will be forever remembered for his appalling miss against France at Wembley in 1992. Clean through on goal with only the keeper to beat, his attempted chip (was it?) ended up closer to the corner flag than the goal. Embarrassing.

Best quote: 'When Geoff Thomas traps the ball it goes as far as I used to kick it.' – George Best

In an all white strip, Carlton looked like a goalpost

CARLTON PALMER

18 caps, 1992-94, 1 goal

This willing workhorse was perhaps the most criticised of Graham Taylor's many dodgy selections during the early Nineties. It's not that he's a bad player – he's just some way distant from being an international. Covering the ground like a hermit crab with unnaturally long legs can be useful in the lower reaches of the Premiership, but tends to be found out by top-class internationals. Bull in a china shop.

THE Turn YE

From the late-Seventies all the way through to the end of the 1980s, Graham Taylor was a phenomenon. He led unfashionable Watford from the old Fourth Division all the way to the First, took them to a League Cup semi-final and to the FA Cup Final ... and all this with Steve Sherwood in goal!

In 1987 he moved to Aston Villa, whom he managed to promotion from the Second Division and then to the runners-up position in the League. When Bobby Robson retired from the England manager's job after the 1990 World Cup there was only one choice to replace him.

Sadly, Taylor's club success was not repeated at international level. Yet it all started so well.

England remained unbeaten for their first 12 games under Taylor and, even then, the run was broken only by their eternal nemesis, Germany. They also managed to qualify for the 1992 European Championships, although only by the skin of their crossbar. But, what was worrying was that none of this was done with any style, and that Taylor was already showing signs of selectorial eccentricity.

First, he was wedded to the direct style of play that had pulled Watford up from Division 4, but which was not entirely suitable when faced with Holland or Italy.

Second, he had a penchant for hard-working cloggers over skill players. Geoff Thomas, Carlton Palmer and David Batty were brought in; Peter Beardsley, Chris Waddle and, most damningly of all, Steve Hodge were discarded. (Alright, we were joking about Hodge.)

Then he fiddled with the game plan and formation. Players became confused about what they were and weren't supposed to do. The wheels had to come off – and come off they did in style.

In the European Championships, England played out tedious goalless draws vs Denmark and France, then lost 2-1 to Sweden – prompting the immortal *Sun* headline 'Swedes 2, Turnips 1'. The nadir of the defeat was Taylor's substitution of Lineker (by Alan Smith!), one goal away from equalling England's all-time scoring record, in his last international.

It was all downhill from there. England went on to finish fourth in a four-team tournament in the USA – including a 2-0 defeat against the hosts! – and failed to qualify for the World Cup. Taylor's relationship with the media plumbed the depths, and finally he fell on his sword. His record wasn't a disgrace – Won 18, Drawn 12, Lost 8 – but he always lost when it mattered.

England's WORST RESULTS ever

June 29, 1950 – Mexico
England 0 USA 1 *World Cup, Pool 2*
England went into the 1950 World Cup with real hopes of lifting the trophy at the first time of asking. The USA turned up with the strict intention of keeping the scores down to a respectable level.

For the match at Belo Horizonte, England fielded players of the calibre of Mannion, Wright, Ramsey, Mortensen and Finney. They dominated the match but were denied by the woodwork – 11 times – and by some spectacular keeping from Borghi, an ex-baseball player, in the USA goal.

On one of their rare sorties into the England half, the USA scored. A throw-in went to Bahr, who hit the ball from 25 yards out. It struck Haitian-born forward Joe Gaetjans on its way to the goal and deflected past England keeper Bert Williams.

Some eccentric refereeing and poor finishing prevented England from equalising and so the match was lost.

It would be nice to say it is the only time we have lost to the USA, but that would be untrue. It remains, nevertheless, the biggest upset in England's international history.

October 17, 1973 – Wembley
England 1 Poland 1 *World Cup Qualifier*
After the glory of '66 and the oh-so-nearly of 1970, Alf Ramsey was becoming more and more insecure by 1973. After a dropped point at home to Wales and a defeat in Poland, England needed to beat the Poles at Wembley to qualify for the 1974 World Cup Finals.

So took place one of the most one-sided games ever. England had 26 corners to Poland's two and rained shots in on the Poland goal. Two shots hit the woodwork, four were cleared off the line, and Tomaszewski, famously dubbed a clown before the game by Brian Clough, played like Lev Yashin.

Poland amazingly took the lead in the second half. Norman Hunter had a rush of blood and rather than boot the ball into Row Z (his standard procedure) attempted to dribble round Lato, the Polish winger. Lato robbed Hunter, sprinted down the line and crossed to Domarski, whose shot went through Hughes' legs then under Shilton's body. A soft goal. England equalised with a penalty six minutes later, but despite intense pressure were unable to force the winner.

England failed to qualify for the World Cup. It was the beginning of the end not only for Ramsey, who was sacked two games later, but also for England's perception of itself as being any good.

September 9, 1981 – Oslo
Norway 2 England 1 *World Cup Qualifier*
In 1981 England travelled to Norway for what appeared to be a routine World Cup qualifier. They had faced Norway five times previously, winning each time and never scoring less than four in the process. In the home leg they had won 4-0, and they had just beaten a strong Hungary side 3-1 in Budapest.

Sadly, despite fielding a team including Keegan, Hoddle, Robson and Francis, England were unable to defeat the 'cannon-fodder' on this occasion. Although Bryan Robson scored first, goals from Albertsen and Thoresen (no, we haven't heard of them either) put Norway ahead before half-time, and England were unable to pull it back.

Given that England went on to qualify for the finals (for the first time in 12 years!), the loss was not quite as much of a disaster as it might have been. And it did have the consolation of the ecstatic Norwegian commentator whose victory speech at the final whistle – 'Lord Nelson, Winston Churchill, Maggie Thatcher, William Shakespeare … your boys took one hell of a beating!' – has since deservedly achieved immortality.

At it happens, this win was merely the start of a domination over England that Norway have not relinquished since. Perhaps, as most of their team play in the Premiership, we can think of them as our team. Or perhaps not.

April 15, 1967 – Wembley
England 2 Scotland 3
European Championships Qualifier
In 1966, for those of you who don't know, England won the World Cup. During the Final, Scotland was divided between those who wanted England to lose and those who wanted Germany to win. All were gloriously disappointed.

In 1967 the Scots arrived at Wembley intent on proving a point – that while England might have won the World Cup, Scotland were capable of playing the better football. Their talisman was Sunderland's Jim Baxter, the flawed genius who did George Best before Best himself. He teased and tormented the England defenders throughout the game, scored – and exhibited his party piece of sitting on the ball when it all got too easy.

England, despite fielding 10 of the World Cup Final side (and Greaves in for Hunt was no real hardship) were well beaten and only goals from Charlton (Jackie) and Hurst made the score respectable.

Scotland were clearly on a roll, as no more than one month later Celtic went on to win the European Cup – the first time for a British club. Things haven't been the same since, but 1967 was one hell of a year for the Scots!

Bergkamp scores after blatant handball – after this skulduggery no English club will ever sign him...

October 13, 1993 – Rotterdam

Holland 2 England 0 *World Cup Qualifier*

Despite the best efforts of Graham Taylor, England travelled to Rotterdam in 1993 with a reasonable chance of qualifying for the 1994 World Cup. All they needed to do was get a result against the Netherlands.

With the game goalless in the first half, a great through ball released David Platt on a clear run to the Dutch goal. Ronald Koeman, the Dutch sweeper, tracked Platt for a couple of seconds then cynically brought him down from behind as Platt bore down on the goal.

Koeman was as surprised as anyone to remain on the pitch, receiving only a booking. He repaid the ref's generosity within five minutes when he curled in a free kick past a despairing David Seaman. A second goal from Dennis Bergkamp – after he appeared to control the ball with his hand – merely emphasised the injustice of it all.

As a result of the defeat, England failed once again to qualify for the finals, then suffered further humiliation when they conceded the quickest international goal of all time in their final group match ... against San Marino!! Although they went on to score seven in reply, Davide Galthieri's goal rubbed salt into the wound opened up in Rotterdam.

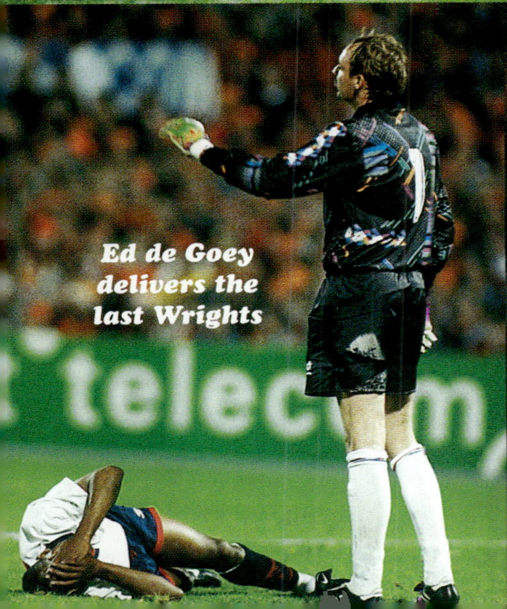

Ed de Goey delivers the last Wrights

You Dutchies may be laughing now, but just wait till 1996

Cheer up, Paul, you'll be playing for England for years...

FOLLICULARLY challenged XI

(that's a slaphead to me and you)

Baldness is an affliction that affects one third of the British male population. It is, more often than not, genetically inherited. It is something that, despite the claims of the many available miracle cures, you really cannot do anything about. It doesn't, in truth, necessarily look that bad. But it remains, nevertheless, an irresistible source of mirth to all (hirsute) men. Yes, it's immature. Yes, it's puerile. Yes, it's unimaginative. But it is funny.

Let's be more precise here. Natural baldness is funny – unlike the recent phenomenon of voluntary or elective baldness – i.e. blokes who choose to shave off their hair. This kind of behaviour would have been unthinkable in the Sixties and Seventies except as a political protest (itself a relic of a bygone era that has disappeared along with free love and a socialist Labour Party), But in the Nineties, it has become something of a fashion statement.

It tends to work for black people, but can have unfortunate consequences for whities – witness Roy Keane and Fabrizio Ravanelli. Elective baldness is nevertheless not funny, so self-afflicted slapheads are excluded from this team.

So back to natural eggheads. We've tried to select the best of those who have been old before their time, who have paid for their haircuts by the minute and who've got used to being called 'Sir' for as long as they can remember.

Monsieur Leboeuf: Not only bald, but dozy as well – spectacles should be worn over the eyes, not the forehead

Slaphead XI

BORISLAV MIHAILOV

TERRY MANCINI
FRANCK LEBOEUF
STEVE BOULD

DAVID ARMSTRONG
RALPH COATES

ATTILIO LOMBARDO
JOHNNY METGOD

SIR ROBERT CHARLTON

BRYAN 'POP' ROBSON
GREGOR LATO

Sub
Yordan Letchkov

Referee
Pierluigi Collina

Manager

JIM SMITH

The Bald Eagle has been in the management game now for more years than he would like to remember. Much respected by his fellow managers, Smith will probably go on for another few years yet, dispensing solid Midlands wisdom and producing effective football sides. Latterly ensconced at Derby, he has shown preferential treatment to fellow slapheads such as Lee Carsley, Dean Sturridge and Robin Van Der Laan. We're sure he's been planning for the day when he puts out an entire eggheads XI. No more combing the record books, Jim, and you don't have to brush up your knowledge of the slaphead scene – here's a team that wouldn't make you tear your hair out.

Jim Smith: The inspiration behind the Millennium Dome

BORISLAV MIHAILOV

When Reading first signed goalkeeper Bobby Mihailov – who had distinguished himself for Bulgaria in the 1994 World Cup – he appeared to have a full head of hair. On closer inspection, however, his impressive barnet was discovered to be a grade A, top quality syrup. To his credit, he never disguised the fact – and on windy days often elected to play tonsorially naked.

FRANCK LEBOEUF

A cult figure at Chelsea, Franck is, like many of his fellow countrymen, an annoyingly cool customer. He is good on the pitch, contributing in all areas of the game, and good off the pitch, where he talks with intelligence and writes with acuity. If only English players were made of similar stuff. Oh, and he has a World Cup Winner's medal as well. Not bad going for someone with no hair.

DAVID ARMSTRONG

David 'Spike' Armstrong distressed thousands of Middlesbrough fans in 1980 when he left the north-eastern club for faraway Southampton after over 350 League appearances. Still, the more generous Boro fans thought, at least the old boy can enjoy his last couple of years before retirement with a season or two on the South Coast. He didn't retire for another seven years – and even then he was still only 33! Certainly the oldest-looking 26-year-old in the history of the game.

STEVE BOULD

A card-carrying member for ten years of the most boringly reliable back line in Britain, Steve Bould has long been pursued by the chant 'He's got no hair but we don't care, Stevie Stevie Bould.' Not necessaily as bald as he looks, but his hairless old-soldier demeanour is more than enough to make this XI.

You can see every strand straining to break free

ATTILIO LOMBARDO

One of the more interesting decisions of the 1997/98 season was the appointment of Attilio Lombardo as manager of struggling Crystal Palace. As a player he set a great example (when he wasn't injured). But he had no experience as a manager and – 'Did I forget to mention this in the job interview?' – he spoke virtually no English. Some might call it bald-faced cheek. It looked like he might sink without trace after his Palace debacle, but he has now recovered to such an extent that he won a European Cup Winners' Cup winner's medal with Lazio in 1999.

Follicularly Challenged XI

JOHNNY METGOD

Dutchman Johannes (Johnny) Metgod brought two principal things to England in his all-too-brief stay with Spurs and Nottingham Forest between 1984 and 1987 – a thunderous shot that produced one of the great free-kick goals of all time, and an understanding that in Holland the letter 'G' could be pronounced 'H'. Oh, and he had an exquisitely domed head.

RALPH COATES

Adopting the 'If I grow it long down the edges it might blow across the top and look normal' approach, Seventies Tottenham star Ralph Coates was forever brushing his (small amount of) hair out of his eyes. Some said this distracting habit – and the hilarity it provoked among his colleagues – was responsible for him failing to add to his tally of four England caps.

GREGOR LATO

The England team of the early Seventies had every right to think that they would qualify for World Cup of 1974. However, they came up against Gregor Lato of Poland – a baldie with pace and flair.

His chrome dome inspired the unfancied Poles to a 2-0 win on home soil. Then, at Wembley in the return, he made the goal for Jan Domarski that knocked England out. He was not finished there, however, leading Poland to a surprise third place in the tournament proper.

YORDAN LETCHKOV (Sub)

With England absent from the World Cup of 1994, all we really wanted to see was Germany come to an early and inglorious end. Bulgaria, a team that had never previously won a game at a World Cup, obliged, becoming instant heroes in England.

The star of the show was Letchkov, a balding midfielder who scored an epic diving header in the match. The fact that he plied his trade in Germany made the goal even more sweet. Priceless.

SIR ROBERT CHARLTON

Bobby Charlton was the first true world star of British football. In any foreign country you could greet people who knew no other words of English and mouth the magic words 'Bobby Charlton' while pushing your own hair up your forehead and you would have a friend for life. Bobby was a phenomenon – a scorer of great goals and a man who, if he had not been substituted in 1970, could have led England to their second World Cup. He also had one of the funniest hairstyles ever seen on a sports field.

BRYAN 'POP' ROBSON

'Two Bryan Robsons, there's only two Bryan Robsons' ... but there's only one Pop Robson. Robson was a prolific scorer who played for 21 seasons and put in over 260 League goals for the likes of Sunderland, West Ham and Newcastle. Surprisingly, he was known as Pop not because he looked like someone's dad, but because of his shooting at the slightest hint of a chance.

TERRY MANCINI

A journeyman centre-half with a sense of humour that arguably exceeded his talent, Londoner Mancini late in his career came to the notice of Eire, who soon found an Irish relative to assure him a place in the national side. He was standing at Lansdowne Road, chest puffed out with pride, when the anthems were played, but found the formalities a little tiresome.

'I wish they'd get a move on with their anthem,' he reportedly commented to a team-mate. 'Shut up, Terry,' came the whispered response, 'it's ours!'

PIERLUIGI COLLINA (Referee)

The most recognisable referee in the game today, Collina is as hairless as it is possible to be. He is one of those enigmas – is he actually any good as a ref, or is it just reverse discrimination? Because he's so unattractive, we assume he must be bloody brilliant. Is certainly quite scary.

PRIMA DONNA XI

Prima donnas on the whole do not make for heroes amongst the UK football supporting public. They jar with all of our popular conceptions about the British game and the people who play in it. After all, the British professional typically has the following attributes:

- *Loyal to the club he plays for, used to stand with his mates at the Gasworks End.*
- *Will turn out in even the most adverse circumstances – minor injuries are no barrier to the tough old British pro, indeed he's happy to play with broken bones.*
- *Is hard but fair; never cheats; doesn't dive.*
- *Loves the game and would play even if the money was less.*
- *Hard-working on the pitch, gives 110 per cent.*
- *Has a drink with his opponents after the game.*

Of course, this is complete fantasy, but we still cling to this idealised picture of the upstanding, uncomplaining British player. Hence, when prima donnas come along – and how much better it feels when they are foreign – we can criticise them all the more.

Let's look at our centre-forward, the much maligned Pierre Van Hooijdonk. Now this may not be a popular view, but maybe Pierre had a point. Yes, he has a silly name for a Dutchman and, yes, he has a rather effeminate, sulky mouth – but he was quite justified in saying he didn't want to play for Forest. Everyone knows they've never been the same side since Jason Lee was allowed to leave.

But then, the prima donna always has a reason. The thing is, he qualifies as a prima donna because his reasons just aren't very good.

Some of the players in this team probably deserve our sympathy ... but they sure as hell aren't going to get it.

Emerson: This way to the beach...

Prima Donna XI

Manager
Trevor Francis

Shearer (right): 'Bags me take the penalties – and if you use my tracksuit top for a goalpost again I'm taking my ball home...'

EMERSON (opposite)

Middlesbrough's Brazilian signing looked strong in the first few matches of his career at the Riverside, but once the sun went away, so did Emerson. English football wasn't what he'd expected and suddenly Boro manager Bryan Robson was seeing one of his players photographed in Rio de Janeiro when he should have been in Teesside. Weather's not the same in Cleveland.

PETER SHILTON

The grand old man managed over 1,000 matches in a glittering career but had a reputation as an overwhelming perfectionist. Whenever he conceded a goal, it is alleged that he worked out how and why it happened and made his fellow players repeat the event over and over again until he was convinced it wouldn't happen again. Too far, Peter.

DAVID UNSWORTH

As Aston Villa and John Gregory found out in the summer of 1998, David can only move to a club his wife approves of. Having agreed a move to Villa Park and begun pre-season training, Mr and Mrs Unsworth decided they had made a terrible mistake and he should have moved back to his old club Everton.

An incredulous Gregory eventually agreed the move, allegedly claiming that he only wanted 'real men' in his squad.

ALAN SHEARER (above)

When Shearer signed for his hometown team of Newcastle, his two main points of negotiation were not at all financial. Shearer sat down with Kevin Keegan and the schoolboy in him emerged – he would only sign if he could take the penalties and wear the number 9 shirt.

Both demands were granted, at the expense of a puzzled and far more adult Les Ferdinand, who happily wore number 10.

JOEY BEAUCHAMP

Famously fragile Joey arrived at West Ham from Swindon in the summer of 1994 and declared himself homesick. The 60-mile upheaval proved too much for

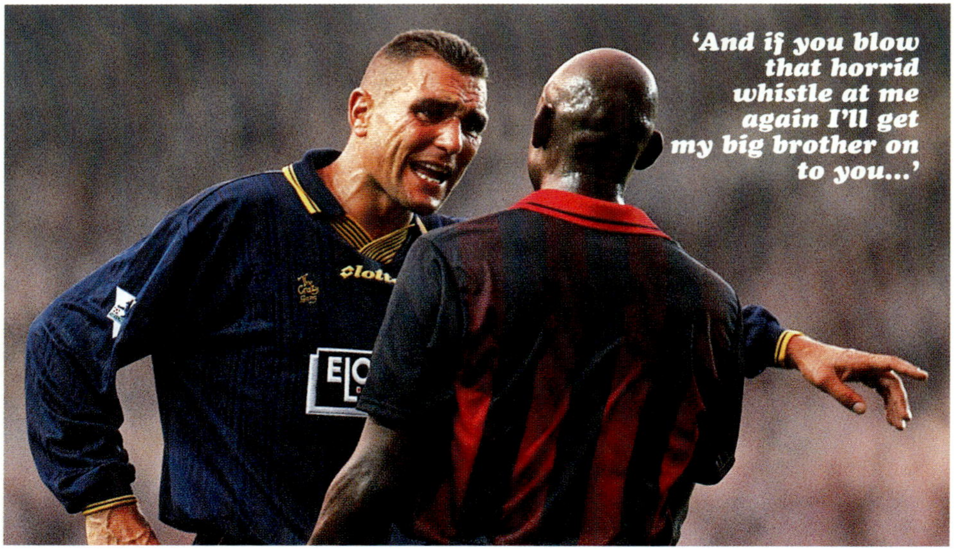

'And if you blow that horrid whistle at me again I'll get my big brother on to you...'

GRAEME LE SAUX

Little Graeme is happily married and gets awfully upset when people suggest that he's not.

Just because he reads *The Guardian* and went camping with four male friends, doesn't mean he's homosexual – and if you say he is, he'll get you.

Just ask David Batty or Robbie Fowler.

When Le Saux threw a 'punch' at his then Blackburn Rovers team-mate Batty during a European Cup match, the look on Batty's face was unforgettable – sheer amusement.

Le Saux: A rarity among footballers, yes he's English and Chelsea bought him

the little lamb, who lasted two months at Upton Park and was sold to Oxford at a £200,000 loss to the Hammers. Harry Redknapp still shudders at the very mention of his name.

PAOLO FUTRE

Yet another of Harry's Happy Hammers, Paolo Futre came with a huge reputation, having played for many of Europe's top sides. He stormed out of training on his first day because he hadn't been given the right squad number. His agent explained to Redknapp: 'Futre is number 10, you have to understand.' He refused to return until the matter was resolved. Harry was not amused.

In his first appearance for the club in a pre-season friendly, Futre cemented his popularity by demanding to be substituted because the opposition were 'tackling like maniacs'. Needless to say, Futre's tenure at Upton Park was a short one.

VINNIE JONES

Big hard Vinnie threw his toys right out of his pram at QPR when Gerry Francis was appointed manager. Vinnie, whose obvious credentials as a coach and example to up-and-coming players were somehow missed by the QPR directors, refused to turn up at Loftus Road because his pride was hurt. Actor's temperament, you see...

PIERRE VAN HOOIJDONK

Known as 'Mr Popular' at the City Ground, the Dutch World Cup striker went on strike rather than honour his contract with Nottingham Forest, who he claimed weren't good enough for the Premiership.

Despite this being undoubtedly true, his attitude didn't go down too well with the Forest boss Dave Bassett or his team-mates. Van Hooijdonk was forced to return to play for the club he had sneered at. Watching his team-mates 'celebrate' his first goal back in their ranks (by steadfastly ignoring him) was truly bizarre.

TREVOR FRANCIS (Manager)

The man who fined Martin Allen for attending the birth of his baby.

The nearest he gets to flying

DENNIS BERGKAMP

Although the Flying Dutchman has been a key figure in Arsenal's domestic achievements over the past few seasons, he has also been central to the Gunners' disastrous European campaigns. Dennis, you see, doesn't like airplanes. The only matches Bergkamp will play in Europe are those that can be reached by land or sea. He simply will not get on a plane. Dennis Bergkamp is 30 years old.

ERSON

PAOLO DI CANIO (far left)

Mr Di Canio looked incredibly stressed when zooming around Rome on a scooter with his mates during the 1998-99 season. Di Canio had been serving a ban for manhandling referee Paul Alcock (above) in a match against Arsenal and had returned home to Italy for the duration of his suspension. A doctor's note confirmed that he could not return due to 'stress'. The British media were, as you would expect, incredibly sympathetic, and their concern prompted Wednesday boss Danny Wilson to kick the little flower straight out of Hillsborough into the waiting arms of Harry Redknapp, who collects precious continental items.

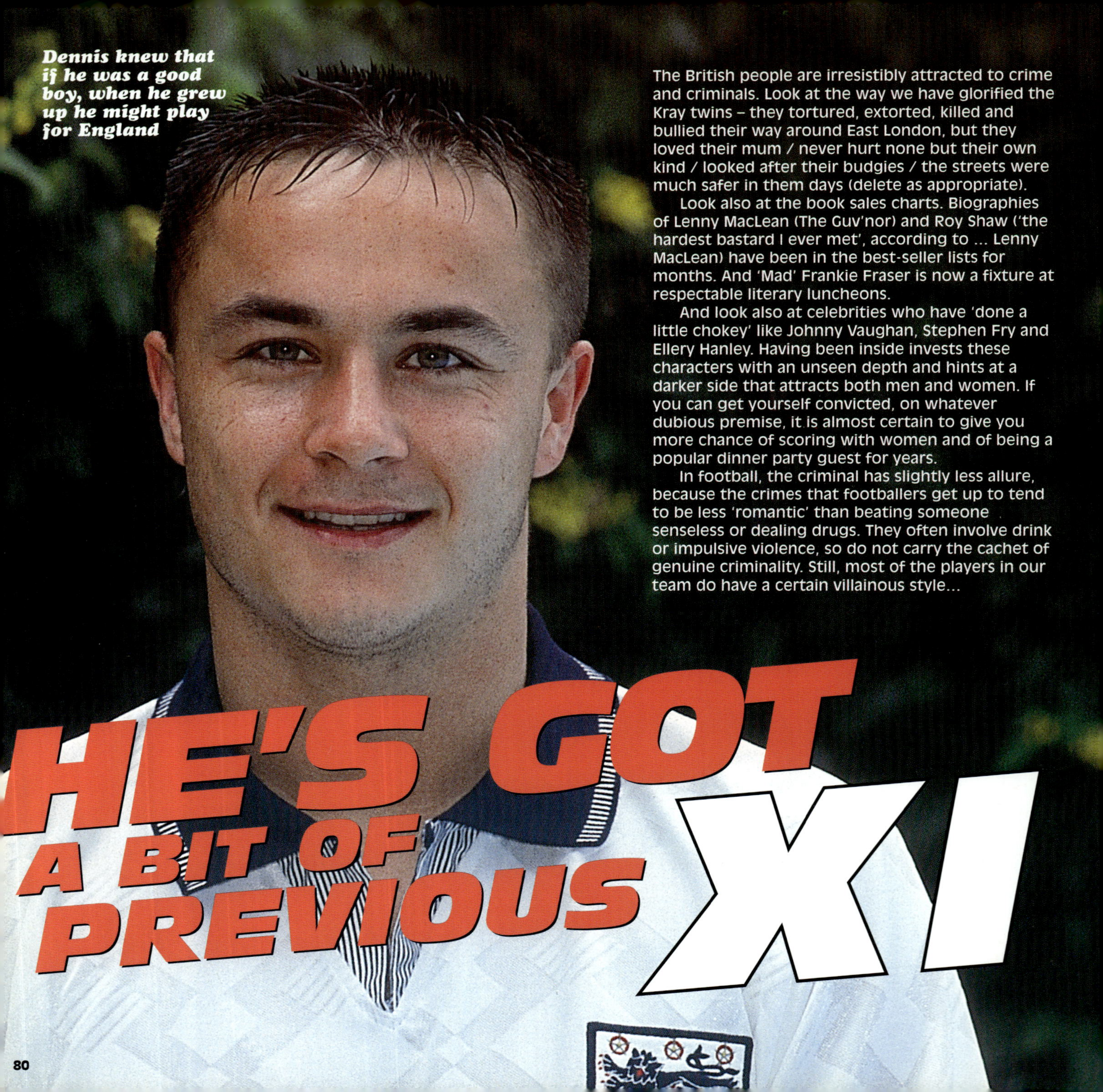

Dennis knew that if he was a good boy, when he grew up he might play for England

HE'S GOT A BIT OF PREVIOUS XI

The British people are irresistibly attracted to crime and criminals. Look at the way we have glorified the Kray twins – they tortured, extorted, killed and bullied their way around East London, but they loved their mum / never hurt none but their own kind / looked after their budgies / the streets were much safer in them days (delete as appropriate).

Look also at the book sales charts. Biographies of Lenny MacLean (The Guv'nor) and Roy Shaw ('the hardest bastard I ever met', according to ... Lenny MacLean) have been in the best-seller lists for months. And 'Mad' Frankie Fraser is now a fixture at respectable literary luncheons.

And look also at celebrities who have 'done a little chokey' like Johnny Vaughan, Stephen Fry and Ellery Hanley. Having been inside invests these characters with an unseen depth and hints at a darker side that attracts both men and women. If you can get yourself convicted, on whatever dubious premise, it is almost certain to give you more chance of scoring with women and of being a popular dinner party guest for years.

In football, the criminal has slightly less allure, because the crimes that footballers get up to tend to be less 'romantic' than beating someone senseless or dealing drugs. They often involve drink or impulsive violence, so do not carry the cachet of genuine criminality. Still, most of the players in our team do have a certain villainous style...

Manager:
George Graham

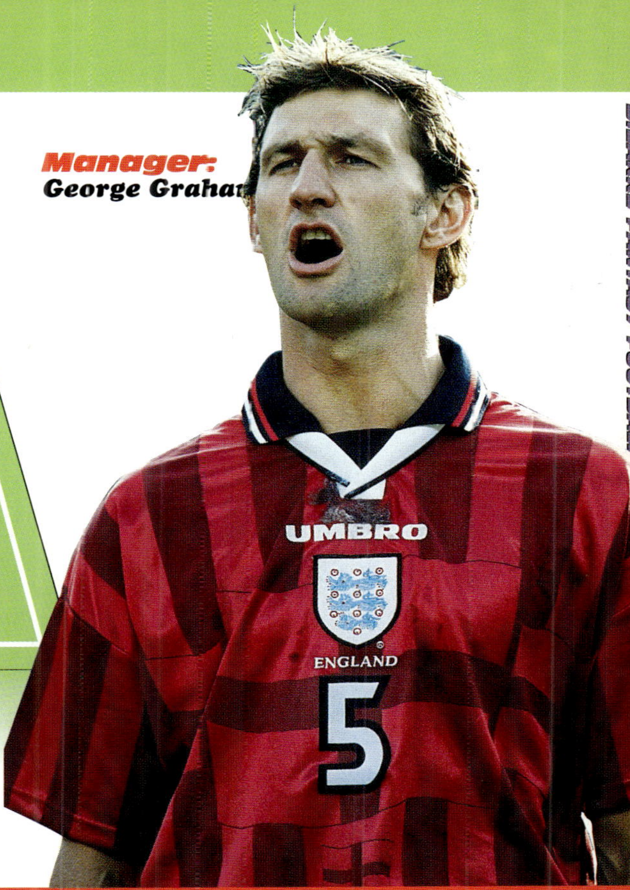

Like most men of spirits, Tony could burst into song at any given moment

PETER STOREY

Peter Storey retired from football in 1977 after an auspicious career for Arsenal, England and latterly Fulham. Evidently retirement didn't suit Storey, whose catalogue of subsequent misdemeanours has Premier League written all over it.

He started small in 1977 by failing to stop at a crossing and head-butting the lollipop man who remonstrated with him. In 1978 he took it up a notch by putting up money to finance a plan to counterfeit gold coins.

In 1979 he was convicted of living off immoral earnings and running a brothel. And while inside in 1982 he was convicted of stealing two cars back in 1978.

He returned to society to run a market stall but was back in trouble in 1990 for attacking a traffic warden and again later in the year for smuggling porn videos into Britain in the spare tyre of his car. As the magistrate sentenced him, she closed with the words: 'You already know what prisons are like, Mr Storey.' A fitting comment.

DENNIS WISE

The hot-headed Wise, who turned over a new leaf on the football field in 1998/99 and promptly got sent off three times, attacked a 65-year-old black cab driver after a night out at Terry Venables' exclusive club, Scribes West.

Wise was sentenced to three months in jail, although he later won an appeal against the sentence.

Many would say that some of his tackles deserve worse, although his worst crime is probably impersonating an England international.

TONY ADAMS (above)

Arsenal have, in recent years, been difficult to beat not only on the pitch but also in the courts. They specialise in drunk driving with Charlie Nicholas, Tony Woodcock, Alan Sunderland, Graham Rix and Kenny Sansom amongst those fined or banned while representing the red and white.

Tony Adams topped them all, being clocked doing 73mph through a road junction then crashing horribly into a telegraph pole and wall. Imprisoned for four months, he returned to more booze before eventually sorting his life out.

TERRY BUTCHER

An Auld Firm derby is a combustible affair at the best of times, but the two-all draw on Saturday October 17, 1987 saw it reach new heights. Fifteen minutes into the game, Frank McAvennie the Celtic

DUNCAN FERGUSON

Duncan Ferguson is now one of Britain's best-paid footballers. His £40,000 per week is, however, a far cry from the prison wages he received in 1995 in Barlinnie Jail. He was unfortunate in that his offence had taken place on the pitch, but he had a history of violent altercations before him. Perhaps the worst was in 1993 when he was fined for kicking and punching a postman ... his hapless victim was on crutches at the time!

Duncan Disorderly

centre-forward threw a punch at Chris Woods, the Rangers keeper. Before you could say 'Mo Johnston', Terry Butcher and Graham Roberts had joined battle. The full-scale fight was quelled by the police, but all four main protagonists were charged with 'conduct likely to cause a breach of the peace among spectators'. Woods and Butcher – both English imports – were accused of acting more Scots than the Scots, found guilty and fined.

MICKEY THOMAS

In 1992, Mickey Thomas was seeing out his career at his first club, Wrexham, where part of his role was to look after the YTS trainees. He clearly took his responsibilities seriously, providing the players with £10 and £20 notes, which he sold them for a fiver, to enjoy their nights on the town. The only problem was that the notes were forged, and Thomas was caught and sentenced to 18 months in jail. On his way into court he had joked with reporters, saying: 'Anyone got change for a tenner for the phone?' He probably regretted that afterwards.

JAN MOLBY

The great white one ended up in jail after clocking up over 100mph in a built-up area, driving on the wrong side of the road, speeding through numerous red lights and playing chicken with a police car coming towards him. All this with three passengers! So dangerous was his driving, the police actually gave up the chase. The result – three months in jail and sentenced to a Scouse accent.

CHARLIE NICHOLAS

One of the great scandals of Scottish football in the mid-1980s was 'the case of the stolen chip'. On holiday in Ibiza, Charlie Nicholas allegedly tried to steal a chip from a holiday-maker outside a bar. The holiday-maker in question, a 28-year-old girl away with her boyfriend, told Nicholas to go away – thus provoking a violent assault from the footballer. Nicholas has always disputed the severity of the incident, but settled for what was then a large sum of money. Perhaps he wanted to prevent more stories of his white leather suits coming into the public eye.

GEORGE BEST

George Best, it is fair to say, has a drinking problem. After one of his many attempts to dry out in 1984 he began drinking again with a vengeance. Arrested for drink-driving in November, he was charged to appear at Bow Street Magistrates' Court next day. When he didn't show up, the police went round to get him. In his drunken stupor, Best did a runner and it took 20 policeman to find him, catch him and contain him. Two months inside and yet another chapter in the Best legend.

GEORGE GRAHAM (Manager)

Bungs are nothing new in football – they have been used to reward managers and intermediaries for clinching transfer deals for years. At Arsenal, George Graham appeared to treat them as an art form. His signings of Anders Limpar, John Jensen and the utterly useless Pal Lydersen resulted in him receiving over £400,000 from agent Rune Hauge. Though Graham gave the money back (after his 'gifts' had become public knowledge), he was banned from football for a year. Amazingly, he is still idolised by Arsenal fans.

Things football clubs say when their players are in prison

'He's away on missionary work in China.'

'He's detained at Her Majesty's Pleasure/banged up/doing bird/in chokey.'

'He's paying his debt to society.'

'He's being buggered senseless by a 6'6" skinhead.'

Tony's testimonial game was not exactly a sell out

TONY KAY

Perhaps the most infamous episode in the history of football in England was the match-fixing scandal of the early 1960s. The revelations of Jimmy Gauld, a former Everton and Charlton forward, lifted the lid on a practice that many had suspected but which had never been proved, and that shook the game to its very foundations. Gauld revealed that games were being fixed across the country and as many as 60 players were implicated.

The two biggest casualties were the Sheffield Wednesday duo of Peter Swan and Tony Kay. Swan already had 19 caps to his name, while Kay was an up-and-coming midfielder much fancied for a place in the 1966 World Cup squad. They had thrown a game against Ipswich in return for £100 in betting winnings. For this they, along with eight other players, including Gauld himself, were jailed and banned from the game for life.

Rene Higuita The Scorpio,

South America has over the years produced many, let us say, unusual goalkeepers. From Peru, there was Ramon Quiroga – also known as El Loco – who in the 1978 World Cup brought down Poland's Gregor Lato … with a rugby tackle … in the Poland half!! Mexico gave us Jorge Campos – he of the loud shirts – who gets bored playing in goal so plays alternate weeks at centre-forward. And Paraguay has Jose Chilavert, the team's captain who, with his wicked swerving free kicks, has become one of his side's leading scorers.

But Higuita tops them all. He sports a haircut that can only have come from a rare species of Colombian poodle. His goalkeeping is by turns flamboyant, spectacular and catastrophic. And he has spent time inside.

Befriended by Colombia's most notorious drug villain, Pablo Escobar, Higuita somehow found himself the go-between in a high-profile kidnap release. For his role in this he received $50,000 and seven months in jail, although he was never formally tried.

He proclaimed his innocence throughout but missed the 1994 World Cup and looked like he might never play again for his country. He bounced back, however, and returned to perform the astounding Scorpion kick at Wembley.

As Higuita himself said: 'Don't try it at home, kids, you could end up giving yourself a nasty injury.'

FILI

What a WASTE OF MONEY XI

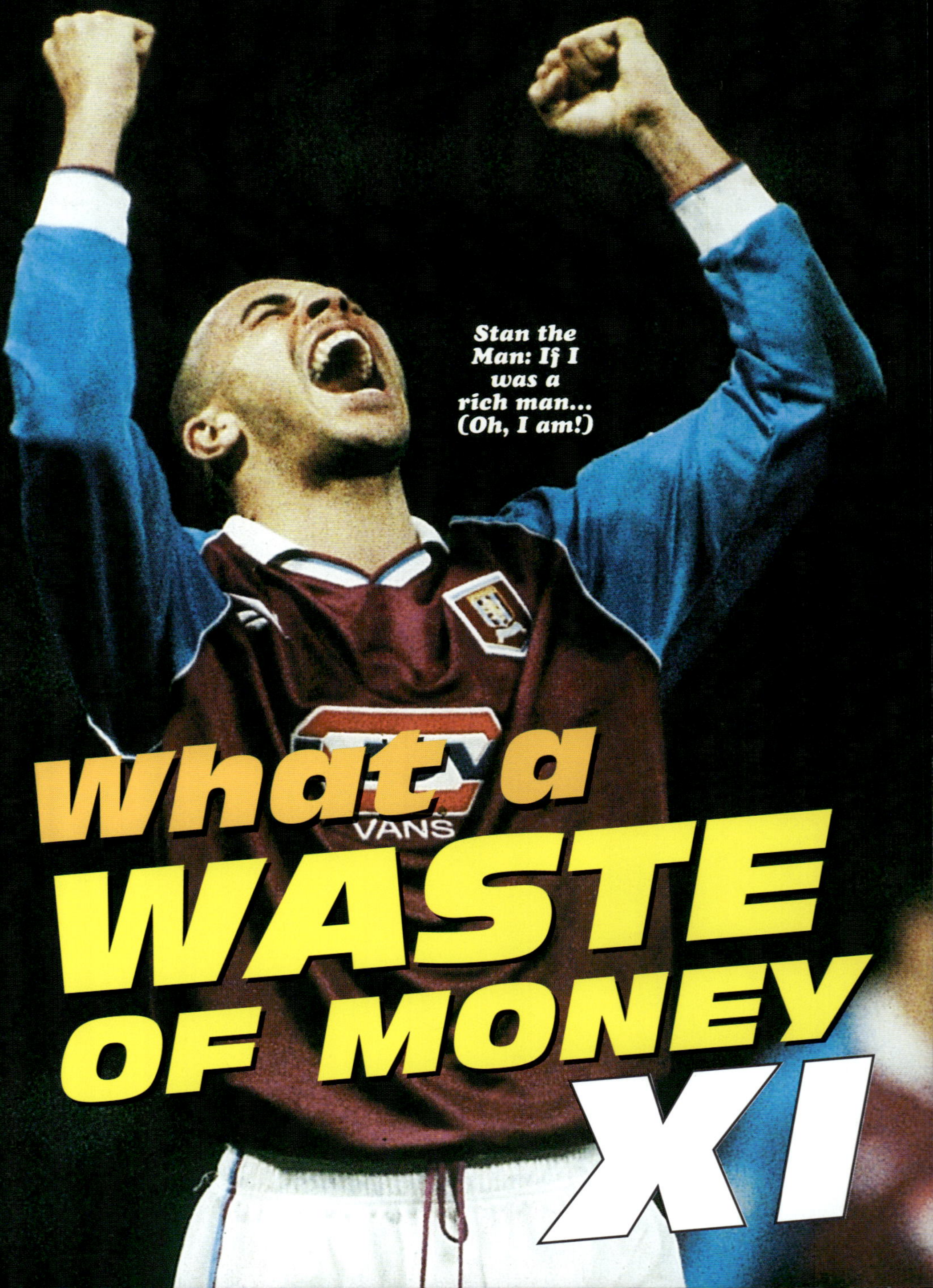

Stan the Man: If I was a rich man... (Oh, I am!)

Ever since Alf Common was signed for the then record sum of £1,000 in 1905, the pubs and clubs of England have reverberated to the sound of punters muttering into their beers and to anyone else who will listen the words 'Why did we spend that much on that twat?'.

Every club, from the smallest to the biggest, has had one. The much-coveted promising youngster who matures into another Peter Marinello; the 30-year-old England international who turns out to have incurable drink and gambling problems; or the guy who looked great at Nottingham Forest but was seemingly incapable of playing to park standard anywhere else (viz Birtles, Davenport, Clough Jr, etc)

It causes great pain to all of us. We not only bemoan the senseless waste of money, but also invariably look across to our nearest rivals who have managed to pick up the player of the season on a free. In some cases we've actually been the idiots that sold him to them. Example – in 1986 West Brom probably thought they were doing some decent business when they sold 21-year-old Steve Bull to Wolves for £35,000. Three hundred goals later they were probably beginning to regret the deal.

However, to balance disappointments like these, there's always the chance that you'll put one over the opposition. When West Ham sold John Hartson to Wimbledon in 1999, East End fans reacted as though their team had won the League. There were street parties, a civic reception and a rush of parents calling their new-borns Joe in a sign of appreciation. So, it's not all bad news.

Alf Common, as it happens, was not a disaster, scoring regularly and keeping Boro in the top flight throughout his six years at the club. But many others subsequently have not been so successful. We celebrate eleven of the best in this chapter.

Subs bench:
Peter Marinello

Sasa Curcic: Another great Aston Villa investment

JASON McATEER

£4m Liverpool to Blackburn 1998

Brian Kidd's introduction to management has been unhappy, to say the least. Inheriting a team worth near on £30m already, Kidd spent a further £18m to guarantee against relegation. Sadly, apart from Gazza getting booked every other game, there are no guarantees in football. Essentially a lightweight, it was obvious that McAteer was never going to save Blackburn's bacon, and he didn't.

PHIL BABB

£3.6m Coventry to Liverpool 1994

The once impregnable Liverpool defence is now but a shadow of its former self. One of the reasons is Babb, a defender who manages to make every position in the back four look like 'out of position'. The hapless Babb is a bit like an Easter egg – looks great on the outside, delivers little once you get beneath the surface.

STAN COLLYMORE

£7.5m Forest to Liverpool 1995; £6m Liverpool to Villa 1997

Stanley Victor Collymore is a complex character – he has a job that most men would give their right (alright, the left is less of a sacrifice) arm for, earns more in a week than most of us earn in a year, and has shagged Ulrika Jonsson ... and still he is depressed. Aah, diddums. Whatever your take on Stan, you can't help feeling sorry for John Gregory. Six million quid for bugger-all! Sometimes life isn't fair, is it?

STEVE DALEY

£1.3m Wolves to Manchester City 1978

The original 'I don't f***ing believe it' transfer, Daley was signed for a then British record in 1978 by the profligate Malcolm Allison. No one but the big-spending Allison could see the point, and most football pundits predicted failure. Daley didn't disappoint, and after a couple of spells in the football graveyard that was the USA, ended up at non-League Kettering Town.

SASA CURCIC

£4m Bolton to Aston Villa 1997

Things started looking down for Curcic as soon as he made the move from Bolton to Villa in 1997. Twenty-nine games and no goals later, Curcic departed to Crystal Palace for the princely sum of £1m. A pretty poor return on investment for Villa chairman Doug Ellis.

Curcic was last seen protesting in defence of Slobodan Milosevic ... mmm, interesting position to take, Sasa.

LEE SHARPE

£4.5m Manchester United to Leeds 1997

It was always a little risky buying a player with allegedly antisocial habits, but Sharpe actually finished top scorer in his first season with Leeds. Mind you, five (repeat, five) goals was not the hardest target to reach! A cruciate

John Hartson looking every inch an athlete

JOHN HARTSON

£7.5m West Ham to Wimbledon 1999

Mmmmmmm. The only possible explanation for this outrageous fee was that Wimbledon paid by the kilogram. Otherwise a clear case of West Ham 1 Wimbledon 0.

Hartson increasingly looks like a Sunday league clogger who has materialised, Star Trek-like, into an environment that is totally alien to him. Mysterious.

ligament injury meant no appearances in 1997/98 followed by a loan spell to Sampdoria then a free to Bradford.

Let's hope he does come back, as he is a nice lad and has a great 'Elvis' goal celebration.

PAUL WARHURST

£2.7m Sheffield Wednesday to Blackburn 1993

Paul Warhurst was a central defender for Wednesday until an injury crisis meant he was pushed forward into attack. A spree of goals misled other clubs into thinking he was actualy a centre-forward, and Blackburn won the race to sign him.

They soon regretted it as the goals dried up and Warhurst suffered a run of injuries that would not have been out of place on Evil Kneivel. A decent player, but an awful waste of money.

ROBERT FLECK

£2.1m Norwich to Chelsea 1992

Robert Fleck's transfer from Norwich to Chelsea in 1992 was famously bad. A free-scoring forward for Norwich, Fleck suffered an alarming loss of form and confidence on arriving at Stamford Bridge and his three goals in 40 games meant a worse return than shares in Eurotunnel.

It's possible that Fleck's chaotic personal and financial affairs may have contributed – at one stage in his Norwich career he was allowed to take home only £29 of his £1,000 per week salary to prevent him frittering the rest of it away.

RAMON VEGA

£3.75m Cagliari to Spurs 1997

A Swiss international, 'Simone' Vega arrived at Tottenham with a reputation as a goal-scoring centre-half. Goal-scoring he may be, but centre-half he most certainly is not. A quality own goal at the start of the 1997/98 season demonstrated his principal quality, albeit at the wrong end. It remains a mystery why he has yet to be shown the door by 'ruthless' George Graham, but it can only be a matter of time.

PETER MARINELLO (Sub)

£100,000 Hibs to Arsenal 1970

In 1970, a hundred grand was a lot of money to pay for a footballer. It was a fortune for a teenager. Peter Marinello, with his boyish good looks and flamboyant skills, had been dubbed the Scottish George Best.

Marinello's arrival at Arsenal was greeted like the second coming, and he was swamped by media attention. Sadly he failed to live up to his early promise and was transferred to lowly Portsmouth after just 38 games.

His career never recovered and he disappeared into obscurity.

Ramon Vega: Peaked in Switzerland, troughed at Spurs

DAVE BEASANT

£725,000 Newcastle to Chelsea 1989

OK, so this wasn't a vast sum of money, and he has performed pretty well both before and since, but Beasant's four-year spell at Chelsea was beset by errors and mishaps. The low point was having to miss the first few weeks of the 1993/94 season – the goalkeeper had his foot in plaster after dropping a jar of salad cream on his big toe.

Another fine example of Dave shepherding the ball into the back of the net

Hey BIG Spenders

Managers who just love to flash the cash

There are few things that unite the footballing public as much as the demise of a free-spending team. Supporters of small and large clubs alike delight in telling each that 'money can't buy success', even though they know, sadly, that it normally does.

The team that has attracted the most 'I told you so' gloating in recent seasons is, of course, Blackburn – champions in 1994/95 and relegated four years later after a spending spree that would have shocked Imelda Marcos. Between Roy Hodgson and Brian Kidd nearly £40 million was spent on such stars as Kevin Davies (2 goals – £7.5 million), Nathan Blake (3 goals – £4.2 million), Ashley Ward, Matt Jansen and Lee Carsley. Brian ... they saw you coming, mate.

But Brian Kidd is not the first manager to act like a kid with a gold Amex card in a toy shop. He follows in a long line of profligate managers, men who have sought to disguise their lack of true footballing nous by pursuing a strategy of spend, spend, spend.

In the Seventies we had Malcolm Allison, the prince of flash, a once-great coach who by the end of the decade had lost it but was nevertheless employed for a second spell by Manchester City. In the space of a year he managed to buy Steve McKenzie, a teenager who had not played a first team match, for £250,000; Kevin Reeves, a moderate forward from Norwich, for £1.25 million; and Steve Daley, star of our What A Waste Of Money XI, from Wolves for £1.3 million.

Strangely, Man City did not win anything and Big Mal was later discovered to have been having a larf! Still, he left the club in safe hands ... they gave the job next to John Bond.

We also had Big Ron Atkinson, a man whose response to most footballing situations is to buy another player. In his spell at Man U in the early Eighties, he spent lavishly, making some great buys – Bryan Robson for a then record £1.5 million – but also some more dubious ones, including John Gidman and Remi Moses. Tommy Docherty famously said of the Moses deal, 'Atkinson paid £500,000 for Remi Moses? You could buy the original Moses for half a million.' Atkinson never won much – he was always more fond of gold than silverware (boom boom) – but along with Docherty provided most of the gags going in football.

Another gag-meister was Barry Fry, whose transfer dealings at Birmingham City from 1993 to 1996 created all sorts of records. Never a proponent of the settled side, Fry used 37 players in winning promotion in 1994/95, and 47 – a record – in finishing 15th in Division 1 in 1995/96. Players referred to each other as 'You over there' and got used to entering the club through a revolving door.

Eventually Fry exited through the same door when the management discovered that an entire team with substitutes had been locked in a training room for three weeks without Fry noticing.

Nowadays most managers are free-spending, and all have made at least one horrible gaffe. The last word here should go to Harry Redknapp, a man who has made more than his fair share – talking about Marco Boogers, he lamented: 'If players can tie up their bootlaces these days they seem to be worth a million pounds. I got one who can't even tie up his laces.'

Ron could not resist bidding for players – especially as each new signing meant the glare of the spotlights (below). The only problem was trying to figure out what they would all do (opposite)

MAY I INTRODUCE YOU TO A RAZOR XI

A mysteriously popular TV show in the 1970s was *The Onedin Line*, a historical shipping drama based in Cornwall. Although the subject matter was fairly uninteresting, millions tuned in just to see Peter Gilmore's outstanding mutton chops which covered about 80 per cent of the surface area of his face and which actually got a credit at the end of the show.

Burners were well in during the Seventies, but for the most part, football has remained largely free of facial hair. There have been isolated trends – most obviously the return of the goatee – but, in general, football has been a clean-faced game.

Where hair has been sighted there have been four principal categories:

1 The tache. It's been a long time since the tache has been in fashion and nowadays, like bowler hats and National Health dentists, you really don't see that many about. When sculpted – *à la* Dali, Grobbelaar, Merv Hughes – a tache can look, if not good, at least distinctive. Most simply look wispy, weedy and rather sad.

2 The beard. The three main variants are goatee, full manicured and full unkempt. The goatee has become a fashion choice, whereas the full beard is more of a calling. Always rare in sport, its adherents in football have really stood out.

3 The sideburn. Predominantly a Seventies phenomenon, burners have made something of a comeback in recent years. Most variants have been tried, although the Amish/Abe Lincoln look still remains rare on the pitch.

4 The plain stupid. Not fitting into any of the above categories, some people just like to be noticed.

Our team, like a combined British Isles squad, contains representatives from each of the above.

Trifan Ivanov: Not a man to meet in a dark alley

Manager: Gianluca Vialli

Ricky Villa: Hair there and everywhere

ALEXEI LALAS
Catweasel

Given that men's 'soccer' sits behind rhythmic gymnastics and octopush in the American consciousness, the players of the USA have had to try that much harder to get the public's attention. Lalas has set out to create a stir, becoming the first out-and-out hippy to play in the World Cup. Rumour has it that it was all put on, and that Lalas was in fact a card-carrying Republican member of the National Rifle Association who preferred his hair short ... then maybe not.

TRIFAN IVANOV
Axe murderer

Bulgaria's fantastic run in the 1994 World Cup brought one of the most frightening individuals ever seen on a football pitch to the public's attention, Trifan Ivanov. The hollow cheeks, the unmanicured beard, the lifeless eyes that could see in two different directions at once – Ivanov was a horror movie casting director's dream. Not someone you'd like to meet down a dark Sofia alley.

RICKY VILLA
Everywhere

As if Manchester City fans haven't suffered enough, every year they have to put up with seeing their team defeated repeatedly in the FA Cup Final by one of the finest goals of all time – Ricky Villa's famous solo dribble.

Argentinian midfielder Villa had played second fiddle to Osvaldo Ardiles throughout their spell at Spurs, but this was his moment of glory. As regards facial hair, the profusion of hair on Villa implied he was an all-over beast of a man, so thank God they didn't take their shirts off to celebrate goals in those days.

SOCRATES
Manicured

The 1982 Brazilian team may not have been as good as the Gods of 1970, but they had some great players – not least their captain, Socrates. Playing in a style not unlike our own Trevor Brooking, Socrates had poise, passing ability and perhaps a little more pace. What was remarkable was that he was not only a qualified doctor (hence the moniker) but that he also smoked 40-a-day. Now, if only we could be that good, it might be worth taking up smoking.

TERRY CONROY
Ginger chops

At the start of the 1970s, Stoke City were a pretty useful outfit. They reached the FA Cup semi-final two years running, won the League Cup in 1972 and twice appeared in Europe. A linchpin of the side was Terry

PETER SCHMEICHEL

Mistake

The great Dane has always come across as someone who takes no interest in his own personal appearance. OK, so the raw materials are not that great to start with, not least the unique Rudolph the Reindeer nose, but he has appeared to be totally unconcerned about improving his image. In the 1998/9 pre-season, however, Schmeichel must surely have visited a style doctor, for he started the season sporting a neat little artist's goatee. Sorry, Peter, but this was the wrong face at the wrong time – ill-advised.

Peter Schmeichel: Not a man to admit a mistake – but the infamous goatee bit the dust in a hurry

Conroy, a native of Dublin who played in an attacking midfield role. Conroy could not have looked more Irish had he tried – his shock of red hair was supported by two immense ginger sideburns that came millimetres from meeting in the middle. Even by the standards of the day, these were truly spectacular.

TREVOR HOCKEY

Caveman

Trevor Hockey was a hard-working midfielder who played for seven clubs in the Sixties and Seventies and who, despite being born in Keighley, managed to earn nine caps for Wales. He was also, officially, the most bearded man ever to play professional football. His hair covered about 90 per cent of the surface area of his face, and had he not played football he could surely have had a career as a circus oddity.

MALCOLM MACDONALD

Burners

Supermac was a goal-scoring machine who maintained a record of scoring a goal every other game throughout his career in England. He famously repaid Newcastle for letting him move to Arsenal by scoring a hat-trick against them at the first opportunity, and set a record for England by scoring five against the hapless Cypriots in 1975. He also possessed the finest pair of sideburns of his and any other era. He was clearly proud of them, as in all photos he turned his head to ensure the burners were given full profile.

PETER WITHE

Amish man

When Peter Withe started wearing tennis wrist-bands, he perhaps thought he might start a trend that would have commercial spin-offs for him. That could be the only possible explanation, as they looked f***ing stupid. Almost as stupid as the Amish-style beard that he sported through much of his career. Maybe Peter is a follower of the secretive sect … if so, any chance of knocking us up a table, Pete?

A stranger to a comb

JOHN WARK

Charlie Chaplin

There have been numerous crap taches in football, but perhaps none as crap for so long as John Wark's.

Wark, who played over 600 League games in a distinguished 22-year career, was not one of nature's lookers so the facial hair was really more of a garnish than a side vegetable. On Charlie Chaplin it had appeared comical, on Wark it just looked laughable.

ALESSANDRO DEL PIERO

D'Artagnan

Alessandro del Piero has been the darling of Italian football since the mid-1990s – talented, dedicated, productive and good-looking in that typically Mediterranean Italian way.

As the century has drawn to a close, he has gone all retro, taking a step back to the 17th century and the time of the Three Musketeers.

The pointy sideburns and the raffish beard would have looked naff on someone else … on him they looked rather good. Annoying.

GIANLUCA VIALLI

(Manager)

Original

Gianluca, like many men of style, has experimented with various facial hair combinations over the years. He makes this team on the strength of a short-lived but fantastically original formation that involved a totally shaven head supplemented by three-inch sideburns on either side … and that's all. Inspired.

Gianluca Vialli: Signor Style

HIDEOUS HOWLERS XI

We have all done things in our lives that we have regretted almost as soon as we've done them. Sometimes it's been something we've said – Gerald Ratner's description of his shops' jewellery as 'crap' was unfortunate, as were Douglas Hall and Freddie Shepherd's pronouncements on Geordie women. Other times it's been something we've done – George Michael's 'careless wrister' was perhaps misadvised, as was Ron Davies' stroll across Clapham Common. And other times it's been something we've not done – like forgetting the wife's birthday or, worse still, her name.

In football, there are numerous opportunities for howlers both on and off the pitch. On the pitch, there's the open goal that's easier to score than miss; the defensive header that arrows into the top corner; or the unnecessary foul you commit in your own penalty box in the last minute.

Off the pitch there's the tactical substitution that changes the course of the game ... in favour of the opposition; the tactical formation that's easier to read than a large road sign; or the risky selection that would have been better made with a blindfold and a pin.

In British football we have a talent for committing these howlers – and we certainly have a talent for recalling them and dwelling endlessly on our bad luck. A good example is England's Euro '96 semi-final. Most of us will recall Gazza's despairing and ultimately futile lunge to score in extra-time, and all of us will remember Southgate's sorry penalty attempt. But who remembers the disallowed header by the amusingly-named Kuntz? Like many experienced losers, we have developed a curiously one-sided ability to remember our bad luck.

Lest we find this depressing, we should reflect that, like a holiday full of disasters, bad luck is much funnier than good. So let's enjoy these howlers. They might have been painful at the time, but they are a lot more memorable than some of the things that went boringly right. Let's leave that to the Germans.

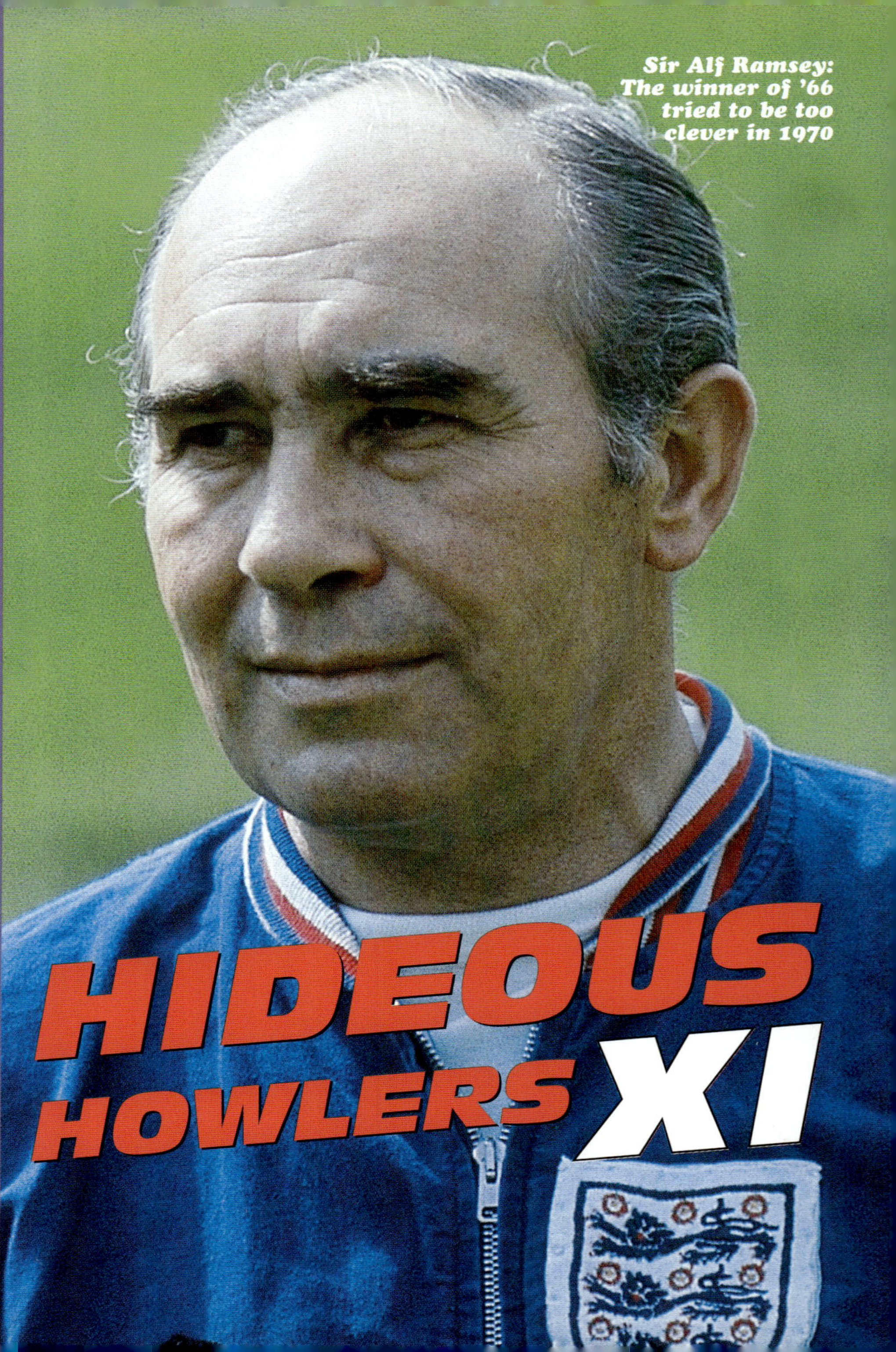

Sir Alf Ramsey: The winner of '66 tried to be too clever in 1970

Hideous Howlers XI

Manager
Sir Alf Ramsey

Right: 'Thanks a lot, Tone...' Steve Morrow of Arsenal rues the moment he decided to celebrate his Littlewoods Cup Final goal with his 'pal' Tony Adams

PAT BONNER

Bonner was the Republic of Ireland's No 1 goalkeeper throughout the highly succesful reign of Jack Charlton. The Irish had gone to the World Cup Finals in 1994 with an almighty task facing them in the group stages. Amazingly, they qualified for the second phase after beating Italy in the opening match and were drawn to face Holland. Without a natural goal-scorer, Charlton's tactic was to keep it tight, try not to concede and try to wear the Dutch down.

Things looked good for about 30 minutes until Wim Jonk hit a harmless shot from 30 yards that flew straight at Bonner. For some reason, the ball seemed to turn into a hot potato and was fumbled into the net by the keeper. It was his last international.

TONY ADAMS

Arsenal's leader of men might be a centre-half of undeniable quality, but common sense has never been one of his strong points.

The England man has always been a firm believer in team spirit. In his early career that might have meant vodka, gin or whisky, but he was also known to treasure the 'all for one and one for all' approach as skipper of both club and country.

Steve Morrow's prize for scoring Arsenal's winner in the Littlewoods Cup Final in 1993 was to be lifted to shoulder height by his captain, our hero Adams – and promptly dropped.

Adams's blunder led to a broken arm for Morrow, who missed the rest of the season. Cheers, Tony.

CHRIS WADDLE

England never did have much luck in penalty shootouts. It's the 1990 World Cup semi-final against the old enemy West Germany, and a 1-1 draw means penalty time. It's a familiar story. Waddle had to score, he didn't. Surprisingly, for a player blessed with so much skill and accuracy, Waddle decided to blast it. Presumably he was aiming for the moon.

FRANK SINCLAIR

Leicester's Frank Sinclair started the 1999-2000 Premiership season in disastrous fashion. Deep into injury time during their opening match against Arsenal at Highbury, the Foxes were holding out for a 1-1 draw when the hapless Sinclair inexplicably headed the ball into his own net with the final touch of the game. Bad enough, but the following Saturday as Leicester faced Chelsea at Filbert Street, his side had taken a 90th-minute lead and were on for a 2-1 victory. Yet again, with two minutes of injury time played, Sinclair headed home ... for the opposition.

GORDON SMITH

'And Smith must score!' screamed John Motson as the Brighton player descended on Man U's goal. It was the 86th minute of the 1983 FA Cup Final and the score was 2-2, Smith was eight yards out and had all the goal to aim at and only Gary Bailey to beat. Surely Brighton would now defeat the odds and take the FA Cup back to the Goldstone Ground! Of course not, Smith hit the ball straight at Bailey and Brighton were crushed 4-0 in the replay.

DAVID GINOLA

Pundits often wonder why Ginola isn't in the French national side. Simple: the man from Head & Shoulders still carries the blame for France's elimination from the 1994 World Cup. In the final qualifying match against Bulgaria in Paris, the French only needed a draw to be certain of a place in the USA. In the final minutes of the game Ginola had the ball. Instead of taking it to the corner flag and running down the clock, he went on a mazy attacking run and lost the ball. Bulgaria went straight down the other end of the pitch and scored – France were out, and Gerard Houllier branded Ginola 'a criminal'.

PAUL GASCOIGNE

You can always rely on Gazza for a prize cock-up, and his performance in the 1991 FA Cup Final against Forest was a classic. Spurs had agreed to sell the Geordie porker to Italian giants Lazio for a huge fee and Wembley was to be his last game for Tottenham.

Gascoigne, pumped up, charged around like a headless chicken. His second outrageous tackle, on Forest's Gary Charles, left Gazza with damaged knee ligaments. He was out of the game for nearly a season and put his dream move to Italy in jeopardy. Gascoigne had talked for years about his dream of playing in an FA Cup Final. He lasted five minutes.

ILUNGA MWEPU

In 1974 the minnows of Zaire – the first black African nation to qualify for the World Cup finals – were taking on the might of Brazil in their final first-round pool game.

Playing only for pride, Zaire were doing well to hold Brazil to 1-0 at half-time. A free kick was awarded to Brazil at the edge of the box. The Zaire defence lined up and the referee blew. Two or three Brazilians plotted an intricate routine. Then...

...out of the wall raced Zaire defender Ilunga Mwepu, who headed straight towards the still stationary ball and booted it out of the Zaire half. A stunned stadium fell silent – then fell about laughing.

Poor Mwepu was booked, but his real punishment is that he will always be remembered for his uniquely naive act.

SIR ALF RAMSEY (Manager)

England's only World Cup winning coach showed unusual tactical idiocy during England's quarter-final clash with – who else? – West Germany during the Mexico World Cup in 1970.

With England leading 2-0, Ramsey decided to 'rest' Bobby Charlton, in order to save him for the semi-final. England failed to reshape and were pulled back to 2-2. Without Charlton, England lacked firepower and were beaten 3-2.

GARETH SOUTHGATE

Due to injury problems, Southgate became an unexpected mainstay of the England defence during Euro '96. He showed throughout the tournament that he was a quality central defender blessed with skill, strength and composure. Southgate never shirked a challenge in any match, but many wish he had turned down the chance to take a penalty during the shootout with Germany in the semi-final.

'Why didn't you just whack it?' asked his mum after the game. Good question, Mrs Southgate.

Gareth Southgate: The eyes of a man living a nightmare

KEVIN MORAN

Moran earned his place in the history books with a hilariously late tackle on Peter Reid during the 1985 FA Cup Final. Unfortunately for Moran, this was his second bookable offence and he became the first player to be sent off in a Wembley Final. Luckily his team-mates went on to win 1-0 after extra time, but Moran was famously denied a medal by the FA's ever progressive rules.

JOHN ALDRIDGE

Over the course of his long career, John Aldridge was one of the most productive and consistent scorers ever seen in the English game. Over 400 League and Cup goals bear testimony to this. Sadly, he will be remembered by many for becoming the first player, in 1988 against Wimbledon, ever to fail to convert a penalty in an FA Cup Final. His failure – or, more charitably, Dave Beasant's save – meant that Wimbledon went on to win 1-0 and Liverpool missed out on their second League and Cup double in three years. It may just be coincidence, but Aldridge left Liverpool only a year later.

Aldridge: even managed to make Dave Beasant look good

Don't worry, Stuart, you've only gone and blown England's biggest game since 1966

Roberto Baggio shows it's not just the English who cock up penalty shoot-outs

SH*T!

'Let's hope he doesn't ask that clown Batty to take the next one...'

NUTTERS XI

'Oo you saying can't act??'

'You don't have to be mad to work here but it helps' must be one of the saddest posters to have become popular in the 1970s. Alongside 'Just because you're paranoid doesn't mean they're not out to get you' and 'Smile, it might never happen', it was sported in many offices – usually in the IT department – and normally signified a place of work devoid of interest, character or, of course, nutters.

In football, there have been several clubs where being mad was not only a help but was actually a CV requirement, and there have certainly been numerous nutters. It's not really surprising. For starters, most footballers combine high testosterone with limited intelligence. This is bound to be a volatile combination in most, and a dangerous one in some.

Secondly, most footballers have big egos. These are reinforced by the money, the adulation and the attention that they get, but are threatened every time they go out on the pitch. When we play badly it simply serves to reinforce our perception that we are actually crap; when a pro plays badly it threatens his whole mental well-being.

So, in the circumstances, we should forgive those who have turned to drink, drugs, guns and mass murder (well, maybe not the last) – they can't help it. In this team we select both those who flipped out and went over the edge and those who were obviously born over the edge.

Read on and give thanks that you didn't become a professional footballer – this could have happened to you.

Right: Ruddock in police line-up mode. Butter wouldn't melt...

DAVID ICKE

The self-proclaimed 'son of god' began his working life as a goalkeeper with Coventry City. Although he had to retire at the age of 21 due to bronchitis, he made himself a decent career as a sports journalist with BBC TV, until he lost it.

Icke now spouts new-age beardy-weirdy conspiracy theories to groups of bored housewives and drunken students. He was described by the *Guardian* as 'a lunatic on the political fringe'. A true nutter if ever there was one.

IMRE VARADI (right)

There's a famous story about Imre Varadi that does the rounds of the footballing world. Whether it's true or not, we can't say, but it gives you some measure of the man's reputation. During his time at Everton, Varadi wandered into the treatment room where Adrian Heath was sleeping on one of the benches. Varadi made sure everyone present remained quiet and removed his manhood from his shorts, placing it carefully on Heath's snoring lips. 'Inchy' awoke immediately, and, in his horror, leapt from the treatment table, injuring himself in the process – and missed several matches as a result. Never a dull moment at Goodison, and all in the best possible taste – just ask Adrian Heath.

Imre Varadi: Will go to any length – well, six inches – for a larf

NEIL RUDDOCK (above)

Ruddock endeared himself to Liverpool fans for ever by breaking not one, but both of Andy Cole's legs during a reserve match for the Reds against Man U at Old Trafford. Ruddock wasn't so popular with some other players however, flooring Robbie Fowler when some hi-jinks got out of hand and becoming the only player to turn Eric Cantona's collar down during a match. Eric's response: to tap his head and twirl his finger – just like you do to the school nutter.

DIEGO MARADONA

Anyone witnessing Diego Maradona's manic eyes-popping-out-of-his-head goal celebration against Greece in World Cup '94 knew they were in the presence of madness. Diego has done it all. Cocaine, prostitutes, fights, performance-enhancing drugs, shooting at journalists, depression, club management and, most tellingly, launching his own leisurewear brand.

In nutter terms, he is the consummate professional. We shouldn't be too surprised. He's been treated like God for so long, he has probably started to think he is God.

Mind you, we don't remember the Bible mentioning anything about drug-crazed orgies…

ROBIN FRIDAY

Friday marked his debut for Cardiff City by squeezing Bobby Moore's testicles. He had 'mild' and 'bitter' tatooed under his nipples. This was a man who walked on to dance-floors in Reading wearing nothing but a fur coat, smoked a ton of dope, ingested copious amounts of chemicals and once painted the walls of his room black to stop the 'crazy wallpaper patterns freaking him out'. Need we say more? He could play a bit, too.

MARK DENNIS

Dennis famously claimed that if he hadn't have been belting players on the pitch, he'd have been battering supporters on the terraces. This only served to enhance his already splendid reputation, gained scientifically throughout the Eighties after a series of sending-offs and violent displays, most famously with Birmingham City's ever-welcoming side of that era.

MARCO BOOGERS

Boogers was a big strong Dutch target man who signed for West Ham in the hope of a long and fruitful career in England. Things got very weird, very quickly, as the big fella found it hard to settle into the English game and become a part of the team at Upton Park. Perhaps in a desperate attempt to emulate his colleague Julian Dicks, Boogers' debut for the Hammers was conspicuous only for his suicidal challenge on Gary Neville that got him sent off. After a handful of confusing appearances, Boogers was declared psychologically unfit to play football and went to live in a caravan in rural Holland (true!).

FRANK McAVENNIE (left)

McAvennie was a lovable goalscoring rogue. With Celtic, West Ham and Aston Villa, he gained a hell-raising reputation for doing the business both on the pitch (with goals) and off the pitch (with Page 3 girls). Never a man to miss a party, McAvennie once allegedly responded to accusations of drug abuse with the legendary line: 'Och, It was only a wee bit o' charlie.'

STANLEY COLLYMORE

Yet another of the game's victims of stress Collymore was treated for depression towards the end of the 1998-99 season. This followed an alleged attack on a former girlfriend, a very real attack on his erstwhile lover Ulrika Jonssen and several erm ... heated discussions with team-mates and managers. Collymore often claims that people don't understand him, so in order to ingratiate himself with his new Fulham team-mates, he brought in some pictures of himself and Ulrika in compromsing positions. What a gent!!!!

Collymore: he'll fight anyone, as long as she's not too big

'Right mate, I'll have the crab pâté to start...'

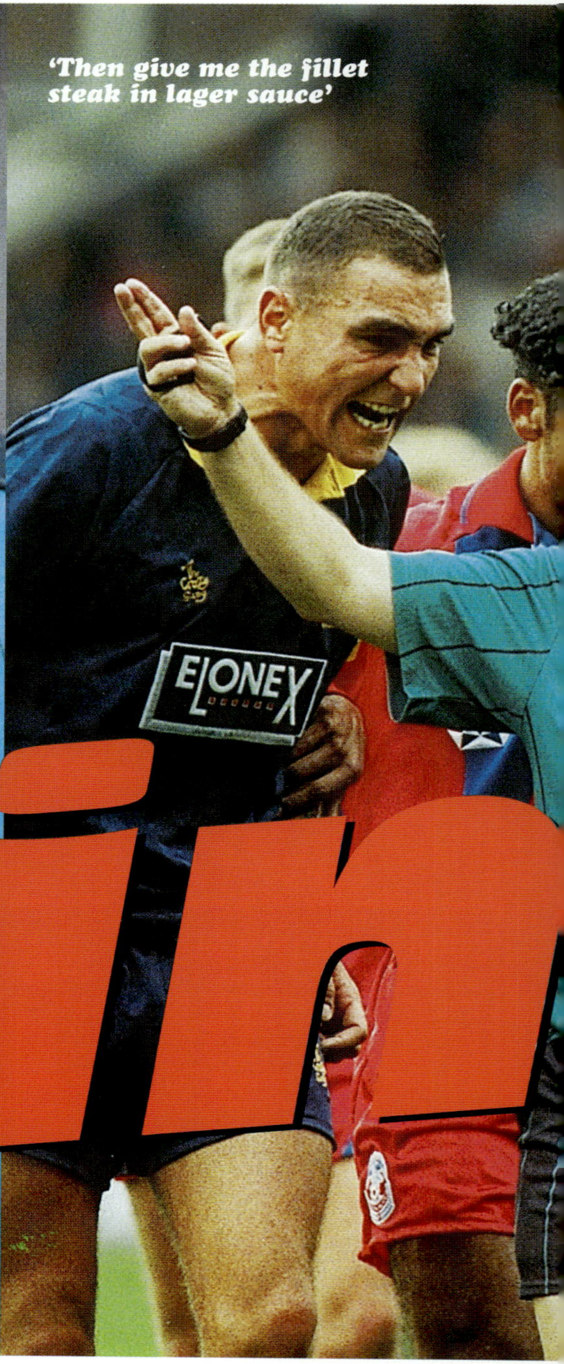

'Then give me the fillet steak in lager sauce'

Vin

nie

'An' I'll finish off with referees' testicles on toast'

There's always something to write about with our beloved Vinnie. If he's not beating up or threatening his neighbours, he's grabbing Gazza's balls or – if you are really lucky (or a *Daily Mirror* journalist) – he's biting through your nose. Lovely chap, bring him home to meet the parents.

FAUSTINO ASPRILLA

A good Colombian boy, Asprilla was facing criminal charges in his home country for possession of deadly weapons when he arrived at Newcastle in 1996. Tino's parties were famous for machine gun fire, boozing and girls, girls, girls but Newcastle was the wrong place for at least 2 of those activities. Asprilla's move back to Italy did little for his common sense, and during the 1998 World Cup in France, in what would surely be his last opportunity to play in the World Cup finals, he walked out on the team after just one match and refused to return. Talk about shooting yourself in the foot – perhaps that explains the machine guns.

The upside-down world of Faustino ASPRILLA

Tino perfected these moves in his native Colombia, to avoid any random gunfire

Player and Team Index

GERMANY
ENGLAND

IF YOU ENJOYED THIS BOOK, WHAT ABOUT THESE!

All these books are available at your local bookshop or can be ordered direct from the publisher. Please list the titles you require and give your name and address, including postcode.

Please send to Generation Publications Ltd, 11-12 Tottenham Mews, London W1P 1PJ, a cheque or postal order for £7.99 for each book and add the following for postage and packaging:
UK – £1 for the first book, 50p for the second and 30p for the third and for each additional book.
OVERSEAS – £2 for the first book, £1 for the second and 50p for each additional book.